Genetics Nursing Portfolios:
A New Model for the Profession

Rita Black Monsen,
DSN, MPH, RN, FAAN,
Editor

nurses
books
.org

The Publishing Program of ANA

AMERICAN NURSES
ASSOCIATION

SILVER SPRING, MARYLAND
2005

International Society of Nurses in Genetics

ISONG

Library of Congress Cataloging-in-Publication Data

Genetics nursing portfolios : a new model for the profession / Rita Black Monsen, editor.
    p. ; cm.
Includes bibliographical references and index.
ISBN 1-55810-225-6 (alk. paper)
    1. Nursing specialties—Study and teaching.   2. Portfolios in education.
3. Genetics.
[DNLM: 1. Nursing.   2. Professional Competence.   3. Genetics.
WY 16 G328 2005]
I. Monsen, Rita Black.   II. American Nurses Association.   III. International Society of Nurses in Genetics.

RT90.G466 2005
610.73—dc22   2004026775

The opinions in this book reflect those of the authors and do not necessarily reflect positions or policies of the American Nurses Association. Furthermore, the information in this book should not be construed as legal or professional advice.

ANA is the only full-service professional organization representing the nation's 2.7 million Registered Nurses through its 54 constituent member associations. ANA advances the nursing profession by fostering high standards of nursing practice, promoting the economic and general welfare of nurses in the workplace, projecting a positive and realistic view of nursing, and by lobbying the Congress and regulatory agencies on healthcare issues affecting nurses and the public.

The International Society of Nurses in Genetics, is a nursing specialty organization dedicated to fostering the scientific and professional growth of nurses in human genetics. The ISONG mission is to foster the scientific, professional, and personal development of members in the management of genetic information.

Published by nursesbooks.org
The Publishing Program of ANA
American Nurses Association
600 Maryland Avenue, SW
Suite 100 West
Washington, DC 20024-2571
1-800-274-4ANA
http://www.nursingworld.org

Book design and composition
House of Equations, Inc., Hanover, NH

Cover design
Stacy Maguire,
EyeDea Advertising & Design, Sterling, VA

Printing and manufacturing
McArdle Printing, Upper Marlboro, MD

ISBN 1-55810-225-6

04GNP   1.5M   12/04

Contents

Prologue
Using Portfolios in Genetics Nursing

Nancy L. Diekelmann, PhD, RN, FAAN
Pamela M. Ironside, PhD, RN

Increasingly employers and consumers alike are demanding evidence of the competency of nurses beyond the basic safety documented by the National Council Licensure Examination (NCLEX). One common mechanism of documenting this specialty knowledge is through specialty certification. Following the model of the NCLEX, however, the predominant model of specialty certification offered through organizations such as the American Nurses Credentialing Center (ANCC) is one of examination. While eligibility to sit for such exams includes prespecified numbers of clinical hours in the particular specialty, the *nature* of clinical experience, as reflected by the time spent in clinical practice, is often outside the scope of the certification exam. Thus the relationship between the theoretical knowledge (demonstrated by examination) and the ability of the nurse to skillfully perform in actual clinical situations is *assumed* rather than documented. Even in credentialing and certification models that incorporate observation as part of the process, the underlying assumption is that the ability to determine the presence (or absence) of clinical expertise is objective, observable, and measurable to the evaluator. This common assumption is curious in light of how nurses have historically criticized the use of costing formulas and workload ratios to determine the value of nursing. Most costing and workload calculations rely heavily on those aspects of clinical practice that are observable, measurable, and easily documented, such as patient acuity and caseloads. Paradoxically, the profession has reproduced this conundrum in contemporary nursing certification exams. These exams attempt to quantify a nurse's knowledge but do not measure a nurse's ability to respond to complex challenges.

This monograph offers an alternative that is grounded in nursing research and documents the clinical experience, wisdom, and expertise of genetics nurses in the process of certification. It is not the passage of time, or the cognitive capabilities of genetics nurses, that have a primacy in this approach to certification. Clearly, the time a nurse spends practicing in the specialty and the store of knowledge she or he has amassed are important and necessary to certification; yet time and cognitive capability are insufficient to reflect the depth and complexity of genetics nursing practice as lived by practicing nurses. That is, it is not the passage of time in clinical genetics practice, but rather the *development of expertise* that evolves over time, that is documented in this portfolio process of credentialing.

Genetics Nursing Portfolios provides a welcomed alternative that reflects the discipline's growing appreciation of the complexity of the specialty knowledge embedded in practice (Benner 1984, 1994; Benner, Tanner, & Chesla 1996; Benner, Hooper-Kyriakidis, & Stannard 1999; Haag-Heitman 1999). Providing an alternative way of thinking about how nurses develop expertise and acquire skills in clinical practice, Benner and colleagues delineated the reciprocal nature of theoretical and practical knowledge. That is, theoretical knowledge ("knowing that") both shapes and is shaped by practical knowledge ("knowing how"). Analyzing the narratives of nurses in clinical practice, Benner highlighted the skilled practices in which nurses are involved (the "Benner Domains of Practice," which are described later) that defy quantification yet illuminate the clinical wisdom and expertise of practitioners.

The significance of articulating the expertise and practical wisdom of nurses in practice has since been extended into nursing education (Diekelmann, 1995, 2001) and staff development (Haag-Heitman 1999). For example, Diekelmann has delineated the "Concernful Practices of Schooling Teaching and Learning," which illuminate the shared practices and common meanings of nursing education to students, teachers, and clinicians. The Diekelmann Concernful Practices delineation provides a new language to describe common experiences in schools of nursing as an alternative to the imported language of higher education. Documenting the practical knowledge, wisdom, and expertise of teachers, Diekelmann has identified a new pedagogy for nursing—"arrative edagogy."

The Benner nursing model of novice to expert has been widely used throughout healthcare institutions as a way to foster expert practice in contemporary settings. For example, Haag-Heitman (1999) designed a staff development program that focuses on practicing nurses interpreting the narratives of their peers to explicate emerging expertise and to reward those practicing at expert levels.

The scholarship of Benner, Diekelmann, and Haag-Heitman provides exemplars of the ways in which nursing research efforts have drawn on the wisdom embedded in practice based on interpreting narratives. Indeed, throughout the past 20 years the nursing literature is replete with interpretive research that utilizes narratives of actual practice to explicate expertise and practical wisdom. It is through the narratives of actual practice situations that a nurse's theoretical and practical knowledge—his or her expertise in dynamic, unpredictable, and complex situations—is revealed (Benner, Tanner, & Chesla 1996). According to Benner,

> mastering content for pathophysiologic, psychosocial, and therapeutic interventions ["knowing-that"]—although essential to good practice—does not address the required reasoning-in-transition about particular patients'

trajectories and trends, nor does it focus on the clinical judgment about the most salient problems. Developing expertise requires recognizing that gradations of signs and symptoms be recognized from the subtle to the more pronounced, as well as the "knowing how" and when to respond. Relationships between major organ systems must be understood clinically and practically in actual situations. (p. 561; reprinted with permission)

The understanding of the reciprocal nature of theoretical and practical knowledge that is revealed as nurses analyze their experiences in practice has contributed to the ongoing development of clinical practice development models (Haag-Heitman 1999) and new pedagogies (Andrews et al. 2001; Diekelmann 2001; Diekelmann, Ironside, & Harlow 2003; Dahlberg, Ekebergh, & Ironside 2003; Swenson & Sims 2000) that are *from* nursing research *for* nursing education. Drawing on and contributing to this research, *Genetics Nursing Portfolios* describes an evidence-based approach to documenting expertise in practice as an alternative to specialty certification through exams. This evidence-based approach reflects current efforts to develop the science of nursing education as well as the science of nursing practice (Diekelmann & Ironside 2002).

Situated in a specific clinical specialty (genetics), this volume provides insights and exemplars other specialists can use to document how nurses expertly practice amid the rapid growth of information and technology, increasing patient acuity and increasingly short patient stays, the nursing shortage, and the demands for caring practice. Genetics is perhaps a paradigm case for contemporary nursing practice because it holds out nursing's greatest hopes for the future—a future free of the diseases and disabilities currently experienced by many patients and families. Simultaneously, genetics raises in many nurses the fear of a future in which human illness and disease, indeed human frailty, become increasingly rare but in which clinical decisions are based on the results of particular testing rather than on knowing the patient. As a specialty practice, genetics nursing has as a central commitment to interpretive thinking and action (Diekelmann & Diekelmann 2000). This means that the nurse acts as a bridge between the genetics scientist and the patient and family seeking to understand their genetic profile. A narrative approach to certification—documenting the expertise of nurses who practice in genetics—will provide a model other specialties can emulate in documenting expertise and subsequently assisting novices in developing clinical expertise.

The significance of *Genetics Nursing Portfolios* is substantial. It holds promise for being used around the world to move nursing practice, education, and research toward greater collaboration, toward an inclusive science that reflects the increasing diversity among nursing specialties, practitioners, teachers, researchers, students, consumers, patients, and constituents. The book documents a new approach to certification, contributes to a science of nursing research, and explicates expert practice in genetics nursing. As the practice of nursing continues to evolve to meet the challenges of a rapidly changing healthcare system, more flexible and accurate approaches to recognizing achievement and expertise within the discipline should similarly develop. Adhering to a single approach to certification covers the diversity of practice settings and ways of knowing that contribute to excellent nursing practice and improved patient outcomes (Scholes et al. 2004). Using portfolios in genetics nursing is a new approach to certification that is research-based, grounded in documentation of both theoretical and practical knowledge while it celebrates the wisdom and expertise of genetics nurses.

References

Andrews, C. A., Ironside, P. M., Nosek, C., Sims, S. L., Swenson, M. M., Yeomans, C., Young, P. K., & Diekelmann, N.L. (2001). Enacting narrative pedagogy: The lived experiences of students and teachers. *Nursing and Health Care Perspectives, 22,* 252–259.

Benner, P. (1984). *From novice to expert: Excellence and power in clinical nursing practice.* Menlo Park, CA: Addison-Wesley.

———. (1994). The tradition and skill of interpretive phenomenology in studying health, illness, and caring practices. In P. Benner (Ed.), *Interpretive phenomenology: Embodiment, caring, and ethics in health and illness* (pp. 99–127). Thousand Oaks, CA: Sage.

Benner, P., Hooper-Kyriakidis, P., & Stannard, D. (1999). *Clinical wisdom and interventions in critical care: A thinking-in-action approach.* Philadelphia: Saunders.

Benner, P. A., Tanner, C. A., & Chesla, C. A. (1996). *Expertise in nursing practice: Caring, clinical judgment, and ethics.* New York: Springer.

Dahlberg, K., Ekebergh, M., & Ironside, P.M. (2003). Converging conversations from phenomenological pedagogies: Toward a science of health professions education. In N. Diekelmann & P. Ironside (Eds.), *Teaching the practitioners of care: New pedagogies for the health professions,* vol. 2 (pp. 22–58). Madison: University of Wisconsin Press.

Diekelmann, N. L. (1995). Reawakening thinking: Is traditional pedagogy nearing completion? *Journal of Nursing Education, 34,* 195–196.

———. (2001). Narrative pedagogy: Heideggerian hermeneutical analyses of lived experiences of students, teachers, and clinicians. *Advances in Nursing Science, 23*(3), 53–71.

Diekelmann, N., & Diekelmann, J. (2000). Learning ethics in nursing and genetics: Narrative pedagogy, and the grounding of values. *Journal of Pediatric Nursing, 15,* 226–231.

Diekelmann, N., & Ironside, P. (2002) Developing a science of nursing education: Innovation with research. *Journal of Nursing Education, 41,* 370–380.

Diekelmann, N. L., Ironside, P. M., & Harlow, M. (2003). Introduction to N. Diekelmann & P. Ironside (Eds.), *Teaching the practitioners of care: New pedagogies for the health professions,* vol. 2 (pp. 3–21). Madison: University of Wisconsin Press.

Haag-Heitman, B. (1999). *Clinical practice development using novice to expert theory.* Gaithersburg, MD: Aspen.

Ironside, P. M. (2001). Creating a research base for nursing education: An interpretive review of conventional, critical, feminist, postmodern, and phenomenologic pedagogies. *Advances in Nursing Science, 23*(3), 72–87.

———. (2003). Trying something new: Implementing and evaluating narrative pedagogy using a multi-method approach. *Nursing Education Perspectives, 24*, 122–128.

Scholes, J., Webb, C., Gray, M., Endacott, R., Miller, C., Jasper, M., & McMullan, M. (2004). Making portfolios work in practice. *Journal of Advanced Nursing, 46*, 595–603.

Swenson, M. M., & Sims, S. L. (2000). Toward a narrative-centered curriculum for nurse practitioners. *Journal of Nursing Education, 39*, 109–115.

Introduction

Using Portfolios in Genetics Nursing: A Model for the Profession

Rita Black Monsen, DSN, MPH, RN, FAAN

This is a text intended for students, clinicians, educators, researchers, and administrators in nursing but it has value among diverse audiences in health care, education, industry, and the arts. With this book we hope to present the reader with information about using portfolios to document the competencies of nurses and their value with regard to caring for patients and families with genetic concerns. We aim to provide basic information about the various approaches to ensuring that nurses are able to deliver safe, appropriate care as health professionals, to assist those in leadership and policy-making roles to learn about evaluation of portfolios, and to outline for administrators the management of the portfolio process.

The Portfolio Approach

Portfolios, as you will see, are a collection of documents that provide evidence of accomplishments such as transcripts, letters affirming performance, projects, and awards. Indeed, the documents in a portfolio describe one's professional life. As such, this text describes portfolios and provides a guide for assembly of portfolios and for structuring programs that use portfolios to recognize and evaluate the knowledge base, abilities, and attitudes of nurses (for example, programs that demonstrate continuing competence in clinical practice). My colleagues and I have responded to numerous calls for a book outlining the process of awarding a credential that validates the practice of nurses through a portfolio of evidence. This text provides a description of portfolios and their characteristics; the use of portfolios in a variety of fields; the development of procedures whereby portfolios can be received, evaluated, and their evidence quantified (the portfolio process); and examples of portfolio evidence (the case studies in genetics nursing).

In this text, we will use the term "credentialing" to refer to the general process of awarding a certificate of recognition of the nurse's knowledge, skills and abilities in clinical practice. The credentialing process encompasses certification, whereby the nurse (or other professional) earns recognition for his or her knowledge in a specific area. In nursing, this often occurs because a nurse clinician develops advanced knowledge and expertise in a specialty such as nursing of children. We wish to clarify here that the credential based upon the portfolio of evidence awarded by the Genetic Nursing Credentialing Commission (GNCC) is the first of its kind to be established for initial certification after the achievement of licensure, completion of appropriate education in nursing, and fulfillment of clinical practice commensurate with the Scope and Standards of Genetics Clinical Nursing Practice, published by the American Nurses Association and the International Society of Nurses in Genetics (1998). This scope and standards of practice document is currently undergoing revision and is expected to be published in 2005. Although the scope of genetics nursing practice could change in this new document, I have chosen to use the current 1998 edition of the Scope and Standards of Genetics Clinical Nursing Practice for most of the discussion in this text.

While a number of nursing organizations have begun to use portfolios for renewal of certification, the International Society of Nurses in Genetics (ISONG) and its subsidiary, the GNCC, are the pioneers in using portfolios to provide initial recognition to nurses for their expertise in serving patients and families with concerns about genetic factors influencing their health. The leadership at the GNCC feels that the portfolio approach allows the nurse to demonstrate his or her unique strengths, creativity, and expertise, promoting empowerment and pride in career achievements.

Advantages of the Portfolio Approach

Portfolios, as inherently narrative presentations of a person's professional accomplishments, are congruent with the essential nature of nursing, which is to care in a very human way about others' lives. Portfolios can capture the values and attitudes of the nurse as they are demonstrated in case studies, the trajectory of his or her career, and the map for future directions in professional practice. Moreover, they document both clinical practice and formal and continuing education.

Portfolios display the unique practice of nurses in an increasingly diversified and highly specialized clinical arena. They allow for demonstration of creativity and expertise in practice that cannot be documented in exam-based certification programs (for example, responding to unexpected situations). In addition, the case study narratives demonstrate critical thinking and decision-making with patients, families, and communities.

As noted in the Institute of Medicine's report *Health Professions Education: A Bridge to Quality* (2003), society has become increasingly concerned about the outcomes of healthcare delivery and has demanded greater accountability from providers and educational programs that prepare those providers. Evidence-based practice is the community standard, and the use of informatics to track care and filter orders for possible errors and contraindications in illness management is rapidly becoming the norm. Healthcare systems recognize the gaps in safety and quality, yet continue to rely on traditional procedures to detect errors and remedy them. Entry into practice that relies on exam-based pathways to licensure and certification does not necessarily ensure continuing competence for safe practice. Moreover, inservice and continuing education are limited in their abilities to improve practice. We are coming to realize that periodic review, demonstrations, and verifiable narrative reports of clinical management may be required for assurance of quality health care.

Portfolios hold the promise that they can demonstrate clinical competence, at least at the time the evidence is assembled. In addition, administrators of certification programs can independently verify clinical logs, caseloads, and practice patterns as well as ratings by colleagues, peers, and employers of the nurse clinician. As described here, a portfolio is a rigorous compendium of verifiable evidence of excellence in practice, capturing nuances of the nurse's caring processes, the efforts toward collaboration with patients and families, essentially from ethnically diverse cultures, and the demonstration of outcomes of care that verify patient- and family-centered agendas for improvement of health. Portfolios can meet all of these goals and do so in a cost-effective manner, especially if informatic technologies, such as online submission, management, evaluation, and storage, come into widespread use in the future.

The GNCC Portfolio Process

This book offers information and guidance to readers who are interested in using portfolios to document the competence of nurses, with applications to nurses practicing in genetic healthcare settings. It describes the various approaches to affirming the competency of nurses to deliver care according to accepted standards of practice, and it outlines the definitions and uses of portfolios in a variety of disciplines. The questions surrounding the validity and reliability of quantitative (exam-based) and qualitative (narrative- and text-based, including portfolios of evidence) methods continue to engender investigation and debate. At the present time in the United State, the quantitative method predominates, especially in view of the policies of the National Council of State Boards of Nursing and the nursing certification organizations. The use of portfolios is becoming more widely used and respected in the healthcare professions, exemplified by their use in physician residency training, dietetics credentialing, and in other disciplines. The Veteran's Administration maintains VetPro, an electronic databank of the credentials and qualifications of professionals practicing in Department of Veterans Affairs healthcare settings.

The example of the Genetic Nursing Credentialing Commission, Inc. (GNCC) experience in establishing credentials for Masters- and Baccalaureate-prepared nurses is explored, and many examples of the requirements that document the practices of these clinicians are offered. Indeed, the processes of evaluating the portfolios by the GNCC Score Team and the process of neural net score analyses add credibility and integrity to the credentials for the Advanced Practice Nurse in Genetics (APNG) and the Genetics Clinical Nurse (GCN). This text, then, stands as a guide for the individual interested in preparing a portfolio to document his or her career; for the administrator who wishes to have evidence of the knowledges, experiences, attitudes, and practices of clinicians; for the researcher who is interested in examining methods of summarizing nursing practice; and even for the healthcare consumer who wishes to learn how nurses verify their abilities to provide high-quality care.

The GNCC portfolio process is unique in awarding an initial credential or certification in a nursing specialty based upon a portfolio of verifiable evidence and in training members of a Score Team (portfolio reviewers, also called evaluators) using online and in-person discussions and conferences that promote cost-effective credentialing. We view our experience as successful in using neural net technology to scrutinize over-all scoring patterns for credential award decision-making, promotion of scoring reliability, and reduction of subjectivity and bias by individual Score Team members. And lastly, we have evidence of recognition and worth of the GNCC credentials by ISONG and members of Oncology Nursing Society Cancer Special Interest Group and recognition of the GNCC credentials by colleagues in clinical genetic medicine (GeneTests directory of professional providers, www.genetests.org).

Plans for the Future of Portfolios

We who are involved in this work anticipate Internet-based management of the portfolio process that would include receipt of transcripts, curriculum vitae, evaluators' documents (from administrators and peers affirming performance and content in logs and case studies), logs, case studies, and related materials via website submission. We plan to pursue automated text-recognition software programs that detect and quantify key words and phrases as designed by GNCC administrators and reviewers. In the near term, we will explore Score Team NetMeetings with conference call and/or on-site retreat discussions of portfolio evidence for final decision-making as to credential awards.

The evaluation of our credentialing program via quantitative and qualitative examination of credentialed nurses as providers of care and outcomes of care (including follow-up verification of performance with clients and families, administrator comments and ratings, peer comments and ratings) merits our attention. Part of our projected operations in the coming months and years will be the examination of the cost-effectiveness of GNCC administration and Score Team operations. As well, we will continue monitoring the relevance of GNCC credentials in nursing practice across healthcare settings: as genomic technologies proliferate in health services, such credentialed expertise should become increasingly a necessity.

The GNCC came into existence at a revolutionary time for health care and for the quality of life across the world. Gene-based diagnostics and therapeutics will proliferate toward greater understanding and amelioration of illness. Nurses have been recognized as the largest segment of the healthcare workforce and thus, central to the application of new technologies in clinical settings. Farsighted leaders in U.S. and international health care have anticipated these changes, and the leaders in ISONG rose to the challenge of assuring continuing competence among nurses by launching this credentialing program.

How to Use This Book

***For students, clinicians, and any nurse planning to prepare
and submit a portfolio:***

Seguin, Chapter 2
   The Concept of the Portfolio

Greco, Chapter 4
   Assembling a Professional Portfolio: An Authentic and Valid Approach to
   Competency Assessment

Chapter 8
   Case Studies in Genetics Nursing

***For the nursing leader, educator, or administrator involved in educational
programs, quality assurance, and maintenance of staff competencies:***

Cary and Smolenski, Chapter 1
   Overview of Competency and the Methods for Evaluating Continued Competence

Dennison, Chapter 3
   Portfolios: Current Uses

Holmes, McAlpine, and Russell, Chapter 7
   Use of Neural Net Technology to Quantify Portfolio Evaluations

Bowers and Spahis, Chapter 6
   Preparing Score Teams for Evaluation of Portfolios

Greco, Chapter 4
   Assembling a Professional Portfolio: An Authentic and Valid Approach to
   Competency Assessment

For the researcher:

Diekelmann and Ironside, Prologue
   Using Portfolios in Genetics Nursing

Cary and Smolenski, Chapter 1
   Overview of Competency and the Methods for Evaluating Continued Competence

A glossary of acronyms and terms is included in Appendix A on pages 117 and 118.

Acknowledgments

I must acknowledge the inspiration and encouragement of two of my mentors, Pat O'Sullivan, EdD, who first discussed the use of portfolios in nursing education with me and my colleagues at Henderson State University in Arkadelphia, Arkansas, and Joanne DeJanovich, MSN, RN, who introduced me to the policies and processes associated with nursing certification. I am indebted to the many members of ISONG who enthusiastically worked to develop the GNCC credentialing program, especially Sarah Cook, Ron Kase, and Lindsay Middelton.

I extend my appreciation to all of the contributors to this text, particularly for their willingness to highlight an exciting approach to recognizing nursing expertise, an approach that also empowers nurses and provides gratification in their accomplishments over their careers. At nursebooks.org, Rosanne O'Connor was the catalyst for the launching of this project in 2002 and cardinal to its successful completion. Also instrumental were the reviewers of the book proposal. For their contributions, I thank Shirley Bell, RN, EdD; Winifred Carson-Smith, JD; Stanley S. Grant, MSN, RN, CGC; Marcia J. Hern, EdD, RN, CNS; Dale Halsey Lea, MPH, RN, CGC, APNG, FAAN; Lisa Newsome Meister, BSN, RN, MN, FNP-C; Judeen Schulte, PhD, RN; Martha Tingen, PhD, RN; and Robert Van Hook, MSPH, CAE.

Lastly, the many nurses who have submitted their portfolios and provided encouragement for this approach have my deepest gratitude. Without them, this entire project would never have come to fruition.

Rita Black Monsen, DSN, MPH, RN, FAAN
Editor
President, 1999–2003
Genetic Nursing Credentialing Commission, Inc.
Executive Director, GNCC
Hot Springs National Park, AR

Reference

Institute of Medicine. (2003). *Health professions education: A bridge to quality.* Washington, DC: National Academy of Science.

About the Authors

Catherine M. Bove, RN, MEd, APNG is a Nurse Genetic Specialist at the Department of Neurology in a Boston hospital. She is past President of ISONG (2000–2001). She is the recipient of two Excellence Awards from the hospital in which she practices nursing, including one for her work on its Genetics Task Force.

Nancy R. Bowers, MSN, RN, CNS is an Associate Professor, Dept. of Nursing, University of Cincinnati Raymond Walters College. She is active in ISONG and served on the founding core committee for GNCC.

Ann H. Cary, PhD MPH RN A-CCC is the Director Graduate Distance Learning at the University of Massachusetts–Amherst for the School of Public Health and Health Science and the School of Nursing. She was principle investigator of the largest study to date on the certified nurse workforce. She has written extensively on credentialing, and was on the Center for Disease Control and Prevention workgroup on credentialing and incentives for the voluntary approach to credentialing of the public health workforce and organizations.

Sarah Sheets Cook, MEd, RN-CS, DPNAP, is Vice Dean, Columbia University School of Nursing and the Dorothy Rogers Professor of Clinical Nursing. One of the originators of the professional portfolio assessment process, she is a founding member of GNCC and co-chair of the ISONG Education Committee.

Robin Donohoe Dennison, RN, MSN, CCNS is a student in the Doctorate in Nursing Practice (DNP) program of the College of Nursing at the University of Kentucky. The owner of Robin Dennison Presents, Inc., she teaches continuing education programs related to critical care nursing throughout the United States.

Nancy Diekelmann, PhD, RN, FAAN is one of the foremost innovators in nursing education in the United States. She serves as a professor at the University of Wisconsin–Madison School of Nursing and has centered her life work on narrative approaches to the study of nursing and to research agendas in nursing education. She has published extensively in the nursing and related literatures, including numerous books and monographs on education dealing with curricula, faculty roles, and student learning experiences.

Karen E. Greco, RN, MN, ANP is a doctoral candidate at Oregon Health & Science University School of Nursing and a 2002–2004 John A. Hartford Foundation Building Academic Geriatric Nursing Capacity Pre Doctoral Scholar. She is also secretary of GNCC and co-chair of the ISONG Professional Practice Committee.

Pamela M. Ironside, PhD, RN is an assistant professor at the University of Wisconsin–Madison. She is a member of the Board of Governors and chair of the Nursing Education Advisory Council Executive Committee for the National League for Nursing. The associate editor of the book series, *Interpretive Studies in Healthcare and Human Sciences*, she is the editor for Volume IV of this series: *Beyond Method: Philosophical Conversations in Healthcare Research and Scholarship*

Overview of Competency and the Methods for Evaluating Continued Competence

1

Ann H. Cary, PhD, MPH, RN, A-CCC
Mary C. Smolenski, EdD, APRN, BC, FNP, FAANP

Methods for Evaluating Continued Competency

The profession has struggled with how to measure continued competence for many years. The licensure exam serves as a mechanism to determine initial entry-level competence for nurses. But once a nurse enters practice, and especially if the individual has been working for a number of years, the dilemma has been, "How do you know that the nurse has kept up with new knowledge? How do you know if the individual is a safe practitioner?" New advances in technology, new procedures, and new research continue to abound in every specialty area of the nursing profession. It was once thought that the life of a piece of information or knowledge learned in school was about five years. This has been rapidly decreasing each year due to constant advances in technology, information management, medical science, and evidence-based practice, making the job of measuring continued competence more difficult. Several methodologies will be reviewed as to the current pros and cons of their use. These methods include testing, continuing education, performance-based evaluations, the use of case studies, and portfolios.

Testing

Testing, or the use of examinations, is one method to evaluate the knowledge, skills, and abilities (KSAs) of an individual. Developing formal tests such as licensure and certification exams involves a rigorous process with many specific steps. Experts in the specialty area (known as subject matter experts, or SMEs) define the KSAs needed for competent practice in that specialty. This information serves as the basis for determining the requirements, which can be further validated through a role delineation study. In an empirical role delineation study, a survey is developed from the KSAs and sent to a national sample of practicing individuals in the specialty to verify and possibly supplement the KSAs already identified. The test outline is then developed and defines the scope and content of the exam. Item writers (experts, or SMEs, who devise questions and answers) are trained on techniques and criteria for developing good items. They then develop items based on the outline, reviewed by other SMEs, and pilot-tested on individuals who meet the eligibility criteria to take the exam. The exam items are then evaluated for statistical performance (for example, level of difficulty and the ability of the item to differentiate between the candidate who is knowledgeable and the candidate who is not). Finally the exam is assembled for administration to applicants. Once the exam is given, the results from the entire exam as well as individual items are reviewed in a similar fashion as the pilot. These rigorous procedures, briefly described here, serve to make the exams psychometrically sound (that is, they must truly and consistently measure what they are intended to measure) and legally defensible. In other words, the exam is designed at an optimal level of difficulty to discriminate between competent and incompetent individuals, follows guidelines as outlined in the American Psychological Association's *Standards for Educational and Psychological Testing* (1999), and will stand up in a court of law. This is extremely important when the exam is used for licensure to authorize general practice or certification to authorize advanced practice. Testing as a measure of competence is also widely used, accepted, and understood by the public.

Continuing Education

Continuing education (sometimes called professional development) is another method used for evaluating competence. It is probably the method most widely used by licensure and certification bodies in the United States for assessing continued competence once initial competence is measured through the exam process. However, no scientific evidence to date shows that someone who attends continuing education sessions or obtains contact hours (continuing education hours) is any more competent than someone who hasn't attended the sessions or obtained the contact hours. This is one reason why more and more state boards of nursing have eliminated the requirement for contact hours to renew the professional license. Currently there are only 23 states that require contact hours for renewal (Carson 2003). And many of these have prescribed the content of the hours required for such courses on HIV/AIDS, CPR, or biological agents. Certifying bodies generally require some amount of continuing education in the specialty area of practice to renew the certification. This continuing education varies from agency to agency. Contact hours are the usual form of continuing education. The following might also be included as part of the continuing education accepted: academic coursework, professional publications, presentations and lectures, research, precepting or mentoring students, and participation in specialty organizations or certifying body boards and committees.

Continuing education contact hours used to measure continued competence have been questioned for several reasons. In many cases there is no real accountability for what is learned during the continuing education session. And in some cases there is no accountability to ensure that the person actually remains for the educational session, or that, if the individual stays for the session, he or she is attentive or even awake! Contact hours become more credible if they are combined with a pre- and posttest to ensure that at least some information has been gained from the session. Accredited contact hours, those that meet predetermined standards, offer some assurance of credible continuing education. In addition, continuing education is viewed more positively if it is geared toward the learning needs of the individual. Some outstanding issues that make questionable the reliance on continuing education as a means to measure continued competence are:

1. The amount of continuing education or contact hours needed. Is a two-hour session on immunizations as good as a four- or six-hour session? Can they reasonably cover the same information and in a way that is sufficient for an individual to grasp the content?
2. Fees vary widely. Does the cost really indicate anything about the quality of the content of the contact hours?
3. Are formal academic courses better than continuing education courses? Is a weeklong continuing education course on pharmacology as good as a semester course in pharmacology?

Contact hours that are provided by an accredited provider must go through an approval process to meet preset standards (objectives, outcomes, process issues, credible providers, etc.). Quality measures can be evaluated before the accreditation seal of approval is awarded. The American Nurses Credentialing Center (ANCC) requires contact hours for renewal of certification, and at least half of these hours must be from an ANCC-approved provider for the applicant to recertify in one's specialty area. ANCC has agreed to accept contact hours from the ACCME (Accreditation Council on Continuing Medical Education) and a few other organizations that have a process for approval with standards similar to the ANCC process. The ANCC Commission on Certification (COC) reviewed its certification renewal process in 2002 and now requires that each certified nurse must be able to show evidence of approximately 150 contact hours accrued over the five-year renewal cycle. The COC contends that "exposure to new knowledge" is important to the lifelong learning of a nurse and to the certification renewal process, regardless of the lack of evidence available that continuing education indicates competency (COC minutes, October 2002).

Performance-Based Evaluations

Performance-based evaluations are another frequently used method for evaluating a person's competence in a particular specialty role, process, skill, or task. The evaluator might be the individual him- or herself or someone appointed by the employer (manager or supervisor), or it could be an evaluation by the patient or consumer of the services.

One form of a performance-based evaluation is a self-evaluation. Many organizations are investigating the use of self-reflective evaluations in which the individuals determine their own needs for improvement and then develop a learning plan.

The evaluation is frequently determined by measuring one's performance against a set of competencies, skills, or knowledge domains. These evaluations are frequently requested as part of a yearly self-evaluation. Individuals may be asked to evaluate themselves against a set of goals or objectives they developed themselves or jointly with their supervisor during the preceding year. Some certifying bodies and regulatory boards use the self-reflective evaluations. The Commission on Dietetic Registry and the College of Nurses of Ontario, Canada, use this methodology (Bradley 1996; Campbell & Mackay 2001).

Employee performance evaluations are widely used to provide feedback to employees and occasionally for determining raises or bonuses. Patient or consumer evaluations are used to determine customer satisfaction in general but are infrequently used to determine individual performance, perhaps because patients tend to become attached to their providers and their evaluations are more subjective either in a positive or negative way. The evaluations may be cumulative over a year or even several years or at a particular point in time such as after a particular patient encounter or a particular project completion.

There is variable objectivity related to performance evaluations. The subjectivity can be limited if specific, preestablished criteria are developed so that no matter who is rating the performance, the same rating will be given. Even this approach lacks some consistency because of inter-rater variability. The more specific the criteria, the more consistent the rating will tend to be. Not only are performance evaluations time-consuming to write, but gathering the data required to write them is time-consuming as well. They may involve observation of the individual for a specific task or over time. Observers must have specific criteria for which to observe and evaluate the individual, and for this testing measure, credible observers must be trained.

Case Studies

Case studies provide another means for evaluating an individual's ability to think critically, to make decisions based on a set of data or a presentation, and to present an overview of one's ability to work with specific situations or patients. Case study formats may be done via paper and pencil or through computer simulation. Interactive computer simulations can adapt to the varying responses of the individual. The NCLEX registered nurse examination used for licensure is an example of a computer adaptive exam wherein the response of the individual triggers the complexity of the next question. Depending on the responses given, the individual may complete the test in a minimum number of items or continue to the maximum number of items allowed to pass the test. Live patients or actors can also present case studies or clinical scenarios, and the interaction can be observed and evaluated, thus combining performance evaluation and case studies. Case study formats along with computer simulation allow for a higher level of critical thinking and analysis and can test a wide variety of information. One drawback of the case study format is the time and expense of developing a reliable case study.

Portfolios

The portfolio approach is one of the methodologies being investigated by many groups to determine competency. This method has varied meanings, depending on what the aims or purposes are, and can comprise a variety of components, from résumés and curriculum vitas to skills checklists and letters of reference. The contents will vary depending on the purpose for which the portfolio is to be used. In the broadest sense, portfolios have traditionally been used by individuals during job interviews. In the past several years, they have been used for performance evaluation, certification renewal, regulation of practice, and credentialing in managed care or medical facilities, as educational tools in undergraduate and graduate programs, and as tools to determine academic credit and advanced placement in graduate programs. The authors have been using a portfolio since graduation from nursing school, originally as a tool for job interviews, but it evolved into a historical document of career development and accomplishments.

Evaluation of portfolios can be quite subjective unless specific criteria are established. Ideally, the specialty organization or entity develops criteria using a set of standards, competencies, or job expectations that clearly describe the practice or outcomes to be evaluated. There are also issues of inter-rater reliability when more than one individual is rating a portfolio. This type of effort requires not only specific criteria by which to evaluate but also training of the raters involved in the process. Training would involve familiarity with the criteria, what the expectations are, and some practice sessions on rating. Another drawback of portfolios is the time necessary to evaluate them. Efforts are under way by some groups to computerize as much of the process as possible to eliminate this barrier. As each of the elements of the portfolio become more defined and the criteria used to evaluate them gain more objectivity and succinctness, the ability to quantify the portfolio will evolve. Eventually the organization of the information, collection of data, and the process of evaluation will all be computerized.

From this brief overview, it is easy to see the purpose for which the evaluation of competence is to be used plays an important role in the selection of the methodology. Other factors include the resources available, such as time, people, and money, as well as the credibility, usability, and above all, the reliability and validity of the method. Indeed, the integrity of the entire process must be monitored and maintained. The next section will discuss these two factors in more detail.

Selecting a Method

An important perspective for selecting a measure of competency is the degree of confidence we have that the measure can perform according to our expectations. Some measures or instruments easily measure knowledge (tests) but are less sensitive for measuring attitudes, abilities, or skills. In fact, each of the categories of measures currently applied to judge competency is likely to have selective applicability toward skills or knowledge or toward attitudes or aptitudes. Therefore, when one or more of the five methods of measuring competency is evaluated (testing, continuing education, performance-based evaluations, case studies, and portfolios), you want to have some assurance that the method is appropriate for the specific category of competency.

Criteria to Judge the Strength of the Competency Measure

Two of the most important aspects for selecting the appropriate method-competency match are the validity and reliability of the method. These aspects are critical to determining the defensibility of the method to predict competency. Defensibility rests on legal precedent and the strength of the psychometric evidence based on validity and reliability.

Validity is the degree to which a measure or method assesses what it is intended to measure. The question of validity answers whether the scores are good indicators of what we think we are assessing (Herman & Winters 1994). As an example, a test, which measures recall of information, is generally not a valid measure of actual behavior (Fink 1998). On the other hand, observing performance or a return demonstration is a valid method of measuring behavior or skills. To select a valid method for measuring competency, several questions may be useful:

1. How thoroughly does the method assess the competency?
2. To what extent does the method assess it as compared with other methods?
3. To what extent can the method predict future knowledge, skills, attitudes, or abilities?
4. To what extent does the method discriminate between those who have the competency and those who do not?

Reliability of a method or measure of competency describes the ability of the method to obtain a stable or consistent judgment of competency during repeated use, by numerous assessors, or with similar forms of administration. An observation checklist of behavioral performance should yield highly similar results on subsequent use as long as no changes to the checklist occur in the interim. On the other hand, the scores should change if alterations to the checklist have occurred. When two or more raters administer the checklist, they should be equally trained to a specified level of proficiency so that differences between raters are not the cause of dissimilar scores. Likewise a test measure is considered reliable if different forms of the test (e.g., different wording) result in the same stable scores. Reliability can be enhanced with a single rater who measures performance over time and with many personnel through training, monitoring, and education (Fink 1998).

To improve reliability of a measure of competency, consider the following:

1. Train and educate the method administrators to administer the method the same way each time.

2. Allow enough time between subsequent administrations of the measure to ensure you are measuring learning.
3. Ensure that different forms measure the same competency.

The *usability* of the method to judge competency is important so that difficulties in administration, scoring, and interpretation do not interfere with the effectiveness of the measure. Complex directions or administration, lengthiness, prolonged time, and readability or technical skill required to take the test all contribute to usability. If usability is considered burdensome, this may influence the way a method is used. Shortcuts and lack of full attention during the collection of performance or knowledge data may provide sources of measurement error rather than representing authentically measured characteristics.

As a final reminder, when a method of judging competency is selected that is more qualitative and interpretative in nature, you are advised to critically select the criteria you will use to judge the rigor of the data collection and interpretation methods (McMullan et al. 2003). This is especially important for the more qualitative methods such as case studies and portfolios.

Summary of Research Implications for Competency Measures

The status of research on methods to judge competency is described as slim (Herman & Winters 1994) and challenged by reliability and validity concerns for the more qualitative methods (Roberts, Newble, & O'Rourke 2002). This area of research shows that methods to judge competency are more valuable for formative assessments (occurring progressively) than for summative ones (occurring at the end of a period) or revalidation purposes, and suffer a universal lack of agreement for the concept, descriptors (observable indicators), and measures (Roberts, Newble, & O'Rourke 2002). Evidence-based questions abound related to methods of competency assessment, the role and standards for assessors, and the psychometric properties of methods (McMullan et al. 2003).

Where research exists, it has been applied to competency methods for nurses, teachers, physicians, dieticians, and dental hygienists, to name a few. As an example, Dennison (2002), in an unpublished review of the literature on portfolios and competency, located 76 published articles and reports from 1993 to 2002. In determining the strength of the evidence supporting portfolios as a method to judge competency, her categorization revealed that 66 articles were based on opinion and 10 on observation. None of the publications were based on clinical trials, and there were no meta-analyses revealing the overall strengths of the research or the evidence for portfolios as a measure of competency.

The most persuasive evidence links competency with testing as a measure to determine cognitive knowledge. The confidence of testing is based on the quantifiable measurement of the test item validity and reliability—long a staple in psychometric criteria. However, when content is influenced by context, as often happens in critical thinking, decision-making, and interpretation, the ability of testing to detect these higher levels of competency is challenged by complex issues concerning the degree to which a test can be constructed to measure knowledge, judgment, and performance. Performance is typically inferred rather than directly measured. Simulations built to performance specifications are critical to ensure testing as a strong measure of competency.

For the use of continuing education (CE), conclusive confidence for this method of judging competency has been hampered by the lack of rigor in measurement (design of pretest, posttest, control groups, and time series or repeated measures). Again, rigor in design is critical to the understanding of strengths and weaknesses of CE as an assurance of competency. This confidence is further challenged by the complexity of inferring that knowledge directly translates into changes in attitudes, skills, or performance. While the CE method may be useful in formative assessment, it is less valuable for summative and revalidation assessments.

Performance-based assessments of competency are strengthened by construction, administration, and scoring guidelines, all of which should meet standards of validity and reliability endorsed by the American Psychological Association since the research base for performance-based tests is not well established (Santrock 2001). Performance-based assessments of competency are strengthened by (1) clear designation of purpose; (2) clearly described, observable criteria for demonstrating competency; (3) appropriate setting for performance; and (4) valid and reliable scoring mechanisms (Santrock 2001). These four aspects of performance-based measurement design for determining competency will add to the source of error or limitations of methods if they are not stringently applied and tested.

Case study methods of assessing competency are in the qualitative realm. Specific guidelines for designing the case study are noted in Denzin & Lincoln 2000, and these are not casual activities. The major research challenge of the case study methodology to judge competency is that a single or few case clusters constitute a weak attempt at generalizing the practitioners' responses to a population of cases (Stake 2000). Therefore the interpretation of competency is likely to be very narrow (knowledge, skills, or abilities), specific, and not necessarily predictive or reflective of actual performance. Validity of the case study for the specific competency, reliability of the analysis, interpretation by reviewers or assessors, and generalizability are all challenges to the use of this method.

The effectiveness of using portfolios to determine competency also depends on validity and reliability of assessment methods, assessor consistency, and the degree to which competency can be established in a specified area. Evidence contained in the portfolio must be capable of addressing the knowledge, attitudes, skills, and performance parameters of competency. Therefore, the strength of a summative judgment of competency is greatly influenced by the strength of each of the parts of the portfolio as well as the expertise and reliability of the measures. Roberts, Newble, and O'Rourke (2002) remind us that evidence of sound psychometric indicators for portfolios has yet to be established. In an earlier synthesis of research on portfolios, Herman and Winters (1994) indicated a lack of research linking portfolios to competence, with only a small number of studies (7 out of 89) reporting technical data or credible research methods. The purpose of the portfolio must match the data submitted: (1) to document growth through a *growth* portfolio (collection of work showing progression of learning or performance), or (2) to document outstanding work through a *best-work* portfolio (Santrock 2001). One purpose cannot be generalized to the other and to do so can be a source of measurement error. Roberts, Newble, and O'Rourke (2002) conclude that a portfolio used for "high stakes" summative and revalidation purposes lacks substantial evidence to support its use in this manner, especially as applied to the field of medicine. Low reliability in scoring of portfolios is particularly troublesome when applied to judgments of competency (Baume 2001; Pitts, Coles, & Thomas 1999; Santrock 2001). The problem of applying quantitative measures to impose a value on evidence that is qualitative in nature poses challenges for reviewers and administrators. However, more success with portfolios has been found when used in a formative manner to document growth and offer reflective content and a subsequent action plan (Roberts, Newble, & O'Rourke 2002; McMullan et al. 2003).

Selecting Competency Measures: Implications

All five methods (testing, continuing education, performance-based evaluations, case studies, and portfolios) have strengths and limitations in three areas: psychometric soundness, applied research evidence of effectiveness, and the degree of meaningful conclusions based on the method, degree, and type of desired competency. Whether one chooses a qualitative method (such as a case study) or a quantitative method (such as testing), the ability to adhere to strong principles of validity and reliability is critical. Our current measures of competency focus on knowledge and predicted performance. Where revalidation is necessary, judgments of actual performance are added to the assessment through supervised and peer reviews. Since all methods for assessing competency are not equal, the profession should require a multimethod and multisite approach to measuring competency. Clearly one method is insufficient for a general sense of competency. Well-designed multimethod, and multisite research studies must be done to reach evidence-based conclusions on how to measure competency. The connection of competencies to patient safety outcomes makes this research imperative all the more important and timely.

References

American Psychological Association (APA). (1999). *Standards for educational and psychological testing.* Washington, DC: APA.

Baume, D. (2001). *A briefing on assessment of portfolios.* (LTSN Generic Centre Assessment Series, no 6., Learning and Teaching Support Network.) York, UK: LTSN.

Bradley, R. (1996). Fellow of the American Dietetic Association credentialing program: Development and implementation of a portfolio-based assessment. *Journal of the American Dietetic Association, 96*(5), 513–517.

Campbell, B., & Mackay, G. (2001). Continuing competence: An Ontario nursing regulatory program that supports nurses and employers. *Nursing Administration Quarterly, 25*(2), 22–30.

Carson, Winifred Y. (2003). *States which require continuing education for RN licensure.* Washington, DC: American Nurses Association.

Dennison, R. (2002). Categorization of literature on portfolios. Unpublished raw data.

Denzin, N. K., & Lincoln, Y. S. (Eds.) (2000). *Handbook of qualitative research.* 2nd ed. Thousand Oaks, CA: Sage.

Fink, A. (1998). *Conducting research literature reviews.* Thousand Oaks, CA: Sage.

Herman, H. L., & Winters, L. (1994). Portfolio research: A slim collection. *Educational Leadership 52*(2), 48–55.

McMullan, M., Endacott, R., Gray, M. A., Jasper, M., Miller, C., Scholes, J., & Webb, C. (2003). Portfolios and assessment of competence: A review of the literature. *Journal of Advanced Nursing 41*(3), 283–294.

Pitts, J., Coles, C., & Thomas, P. (1999). Educational portfolios in the assessment of general practice trainers: Reliability of assessors. *Medical Education 33*(7), 515–520.

Roberts, C., Newble, D. I., & O'Rourke, A. F. (2002). Portfolio-based assessments in medical education: Are they valid and reliable for summative purposes? *Medical Education 36,* 899–900.

Santrock, J. W. (2001). *Educational psychology.* New York: McGraw-Hill.

Stake, R. E. (2000). Case Studies. In N. K. Denzin & Y. S. Lincoln (Eds.), *Handbook of qualitative research,* 2nd ed. (p. 4). Thousand Oaks, CA: Sage.

Additional references for interested readers:

Alexander, J. G., Craft, S. W., Baldwin, M. S., Beers, G. W., & McDaniel, G. S. (2002). The nursing portfolio: A reflection of a professional. *Journal of Continuing Education in Nursing, 33*(2), 55–59.

Coulson, A. (2002). The new commission on dietetic registration/professional development portfolio process: You're in the driver's seat. *Nutrition Today.*

Hayes, E., Chandler, G., Merriam, D., & King, M. C. (2002). The master's portfolio: Validating a career in advanced practice nursing. *Journal of the American Academy of Nursing Practitioners, 14*(3), 119–125.

Hravnak, M. (1997). Credentialing and privileging: Insight into the process for acute-care nurse practitioners. *AACN Clinical Issues, 8*(1), 108–115.

The Concept of the Portfolio

2

Jeanine T. Seguin, DNSc. (cand.), APRN, BC

Definition of Portfolio

The term "portfolio" has been used in a variety of ways, depending on the context. Portfolios have had many purposes, such as simply "container[s] for carrying documents" (LaBoskey 2000, p. 593), managed investments to maximize "financial returns while minimizing risks" (Magill & Herden 1998, p. 573), or using samples of art or poetry to secure jobs or support (Magill & Herden 1998) for the artist or writer.

The most universal definition of a portfolio, based on an extensive review of the literature, is a "purposeful collection of . . . work that tells the story of . . . efforts, progress and achievement in a given area" (Arter, Spandel, & Culham 1995, p. 3). This description can be applied to the multiple settings in which portfolios are used. A portfolio can be a purposeful collection of financial investments, photographs, or artwork that tells the story of the collector's efforts, progress, and achievement. Portfolios are not just financial or artistic, but also academic. In academia a portfolio is a purposeful collection of academic work that tells the story of a student's efforts, progress, and achievement (Arter, Spandel, & Culham 1995). It is a purposeful collection of evaluations, syllabi, letters of recommendation, publications, and research that tells the story of a professor's scholarship, progress, and achievement. It is also a purposeful collection of evidence of program outcomes that tells the story of curricular efforts, progress, and achievement.

In addition to a universal definition of portfolio, the literature was reviewed for suggested defining attributes. Common defining attributes of portfolios are organized (Costanza et al. 2000), individualized (Magill & Herden 1998), selective (Wolf 1989), ongoing (Baltimore & Hickson 1996), and reflective (Snadden & Thomas 1998). Each attribute will be briefly addressed.

Characteristics of Portfolios

The portfolio is an *organized, purposeful collection of entries.* It tells a story of change, usually growth. For example, a portfolio may show the development of a student's paper through various drafts. It has an internal structure that allows the reviewer to grasp the meaning of the story, such as the development and refinement of the student's writing style with each revision. Brogan (1996) suggested having both required and elective content items in student portfolios. Ryan and Carlton (1997) suggested clinical competencies as the organizing structure for nursing student portfolios. Ediger (2000a) and Foote and Vermette (2001) encouraged portfolio submissions that align with the learning objectives or goals. Woodward (1998), Dutt-Doner and Gilman (1998), and Salend (2001) suggested that faculty provide an organizational framework to structure the portfolio contents for ease in review. Costanza and colleagues (2000) saw a portfolio as a managed set of submissions that also implies some form of organizational structure. An example of this would be a professional portfolio submitted for promotion. The portfolio would be divided into sections based on the individual's performance appraisal standards. In academia that could include classroom teaching, nonclassroom teaching, professional development, institutional service, and community service.

Robinson (1998) specified that the submissions into a student portfolio needed to be unstructured by the faculty, allowing the students to assemble their own collections; however, the components of a portfolio that Robinson outlines are very structured. Portfolios submitted to Robinson included a table of contents, an introduction, organized text, supporting documentation, and a conclusion. If a portfolio is to be used as a method of evaluation, certain required elements allow for consistency in evaluation between portfolios. Unstructured portfolios could potentially have a high degree of variability when compared to a standard.

Portfolios are *unique* in how they are organized, what is selected for inclusion and exclusion, presentation, and the expression of the creator's sense of self. Portfolios are individualized based on the purpose of the portfolio, such as for evaluation versus professional display. They are individualized based on the potential audience, such as art critic versus professional standards committee. The subject matter also drives the organization of the contents of the portfolio. Because the items for submission are chosen, in part or totally, by the creator, no two portfolios will look the same.

All of the literature reviewed referred to the portfolio process as individualized, student-centered, and/or learner-centered. Magill and Herden (1998) saw the portfolio "as personal as signatures" (p. 8). Alschuler (1996) discussed the flexibility that portfolios allow the creator in presenting professional competency. The responsibility of portfolio construction and quality also falls on the creator of the portfolio. Several articles also mentioned that the time needed to assemble and evaluate the portfolio is unique to each.

Typically, the more structured the portfolio, the less time needed for assembly and evaluation. A prescribed table of required contents for a student portfolio dictates what the student needs to include and provides the evaluator common elements to evaluate across multiple student submissions. The more variability in portfolio submissions, the greater the time for determining the theme of the portfolio and then collecting and selecting supporting items. Potential portfolio themes could be the growth of a skill with examples over time, the development of a project such as the multiple drafts of a paper, the progression of a painting from pencil sketch through to the finished oil painting, or the creation of recipes with an Italian flair. With variable portfolio submissions, the reviewer then could be placed in a situation of comparing apples to oranges. Consider trying to select the "best" portfolio from a collection of ceramic designs, a collection of oil paintings, and a collection of musical scores.

Portfolios are designed to be *selective*. The creator reviews all potential entries for thematic and/or purposeful appropriateness; just as a broker would not buy every available stock, an artist would not want to put every piece of his or her work into his or her portfolio. The theme or purpose and the intended audience need to be considered when items are reviewed for inclusion. Baltimore and Hickson (1996) identified the portfolio as a showcase of accomplishments. Schilling and Schilling (1993) referred to artifacts, which could be writing samples, artwork, photographs, and the like. Ediger (2000a) suggested that a representative sample of work be included in the portfolio. Herman and Winters (1994) called for the submission of best or favorite pieces, and Magill and Herden (1998) recommended selecting pieces appropriate for the audience. The submissions selected provided visual evidence of skills, experiences (Salend 2001), and learning (Snadden & Thomas 1998). Wolf (1989) suggested selecting not only a range of works but also a biography of works. This biography could include various drafts of a single work, thus illustrating the process and growth involved.

The portfolio tells an *ongoing* story. The "story" of the portfolio could be a professional journey beginning with classroom theory, enhanced by concrete experiences, strengthened by continuing formal and informal educational opportunities, and culminating in a professional credential. It has beginning and end, based on the purpose and the timing of development. When the creator is motivated, either internally or externally, to review the portfolio, the context, entries, and time frame will change.

Most authors identify the portfolio process as active or continuous. Baltimore and Hickson (1996) described the portfolio as ongoing, focusing on growth and achievement. Ediger (2000b) suggested that the portfolio is a mechanism for comparing the past to the present. Karlowicz (2000) also viewed a portfolio as a collection over time. Tierney and colleagues (1998) provided the visual aspect of the ongoing nature of a portfolio by referring to it as an evidentiary trail. The "trail" is created using a set of collected images of the author's life.

Reflection is a significant step in the portfolio process. It provides the rationale for entries, telling the story of growth and achievement. It also demonstrates the significance of the work and links it to "how the world can be changed" (Brookfield 1995, p. 217). Most authors included some type of reflection in their discussion of the portfolio. Some required description (Baltimore & Hickson 1996; Bernstein & Edwards 2001; Brogan 1996), caption statements (Salend 2001), or justification of submissions (Camp 1998; Woodward 1998), while others looked for a connection between information, activities, and theory (Campbell 2000; Foote & Vermette 2001; Hebert 1998; Herman & Winters 1994; Karlowicz 2000; LaBoskey 2000; Melograno 1994; Routledge & Willson 1997; Sorrell et al. 1997; Tierney et al. 1998; Wenzel, Briggs, & Puryear 1998; Wolf 1989). These reflective statements provide the reviewer a context within which to place the submissions. Snadden and Thomas (1998) stated that "it is essential that the portfolio does not become a mere collection of events seen or experienced, but contains critical reflections on these and the learning that has been made from them" (p. 192). The reflection provides the answers to the questions "why" and "so what" that the reviewer would raise when seeing the portfolio.

The reflective journal can be a component of the portfolio. The reflective journal has specific guidelines, which many supporters of a portfolio find helpful. Eyler, Giles, and Schmiede (1996) identify four themes that are can be used to guide reflection: (1) reflection is ongoing; (2) it bridges theory and experience; (3) it questions assumptions; (4) it considers the purpose of a portfolio. The reflective journal guidelines structure the descriptions, justifications, connections, and general narrative that are components of the portfolio process.

Portfolio Use in Education: Review of Literature

A revolution in educational evaluation methods began in the late 1980s. Concern was raised that standardized tests might not be measuring what was really important. "Assessment tasks should be redesigned to more closely resemble real learning tasks" (Shepard 1989, p. 8). Shepard (1989) discussed this emerging theme, citing a sample curriculum implemented in California in which two grade levels used teacher-developed writing assessments. The assessments included portfolio submissions of eight types of writing at each grade level.

Shepard (1989) also discussed how mathematics teachers included portfolios and performance tasks to evaluate the students' problem-solving ability. Students were required to show their multistep solutions for selected word problems. Science and history teachers were also encouraged to add performance measurements, such as examinations and quizzes, to the traditional evaluation process. Overall, the impression was that portfolios lacked psychometric rigor but captured aspects of the students' abilities that could not be measured with the traditional quantitative performance evaluation tools. Thus, a multifaceted approach to evaluation was encouraged that included both traditional examinations, and portfolios of individual accomplishments.

Portfolio assessment for education became more and more popular in the literature. The review of literature revealed the application of the portfolio for student assessment in elementary school (Hebert 1998; Herman & Winters 1994; Madaus & Kellaghan 1993; Wolf 1989; Worthen 1993), high school (Ediger 2000b; Melograno 1994), and college settings (Campbell 2000; Johnson, McDaniel, & Willeke 2000; LaBoskey 2000; Woodward 1998).

Topics that have successfully been evaluated through a portfolio process include mathematics (Abruscato 1993; Robinson 1998), physical education (Melograno 1994; Senne & Rikard 2002), counselor education (Alschuler 1996; Baltimore & Hickson 1996), writing (Camp 1998; Hewitt 2001), business and management (Magill & Herden 1998), environmental science (Costanza et al. 2000), secondary and elementary education (Dutt-Doner & Gilman 1998), and geography (Ediger 2000a). Evidence of growth, accomplishments, and/or achievement of standards has been documented using portfolios. For example, students have demonstrated increased physical strength and agility through the inclusion of fitness scores and related reflective entries from the beginning and end of a physical education course.

The portfolio process has been adapted for students (Mills 1997; Parsons 1998; Popham 1993), faculty (Bernstein & Edwards 2001; Brogan 1995), and curriculum evaluation (Schilling & Schilling 1993; Tierney et al. 1998). Portfolios have evolved into a professional evaluation tool used to document professional growth (Doolittle 1994; Foote & Vermette 2001; Salend 2001), achievement of established standards (Lyons 1996; Magill & Herden, 1998), and/or competence for national certification, for example, Registered Dieticians (Bradley 1994; Smith & Tillema 2001).

Portfolio Use in the Health Professions

Portfolios have begun to be used in the health professions in response to a 1998 Pew Health Professions Commission report. The commission sought proof of professional competence through demonstration of knowledge and skills (Serembus 2000). The portfolio provided a mechanism to demonstrate continued competence. The portfolio process was implemented both in educational programs (Pitts et al. 2002; Snadden & Thomas 1998) and in professional development (Donen 1998; Jensen & Saylor 1994). Health professions that have documented the use of portfolios include: occupational therapy (Alsop 2001), dietetics (Weddle et al. 2002), physical therapy (Routledge & Willson 1997), social work (Taylor et al. 1999), medicine (Dyne, Strauss, & Rinnert 2002), and nursing.

Portfolios have been used in medical schools to document achievement of educational outcomes (Ben-David 2000; Davis et al. 2001) and in practice for documenting continued competence (Chambers 2002; Donen 1998; Wilkinson et al. 2002). In medical education, the portfolio can include a checklist of skills that have been successfully performed, case logs of patient care and associated outcomes, and reflection on the student's practice, knowledge and skill development, and expanding confidence. In practice, again case logs and skills checklists are appropriate submissions. Letters of thanks, continuing education participation and presentations, and peer reviews may also be included as submissions.

Portfolios can offer flexibility to demonstrate professional development and competence by including examples from professional practice that demonstrate a variety of knowledge and skills. A paper and pencil examination, while measuring a standardized knowledge level, does not necessarily measure the dynamic nature of an individual's professional practice. The portfolio process allows the professional the opportunity to provide a snapshot of his or her actual practice.

Portfolio Use in Nursing Education

Darbyshire (1995) was one of the first authors to discuss the use of portfolios for assessment in the context of nursing education. Darbyshire focused on the process of learning rather than the process of teaching: looking at the unfolding of knowledge through interactions with the client, family, and community; exposure to clinical stories; and participation of the learner.

In pursuing education, portfolios have been used to evaluate the clinical performance (Lettus, Moessner, & Dooley 2001; Tracy et al. 2000; Wenzel et al. 1998), critical thinking (Bratt 1998; Maich, Brown, & Royle 2000; Sorrell et al. 1997), achievement of program outcomes (Ryan & Carlton 1997), and overall performance (Snadden & Thomas 1998) of nursing students. Karlowicz (2000) and Tracy and colleagues (2000) gave illustrations of the use of portfolios for program evaluation in nursing education. Portfolios were used to illustrate and measure achievement of program outcomes through the submission of faculty and student work. Karlowicz identified benefits of portfolio evaluation as summative evaluation of student performance, student reflection, faculty-student collaboration, and instructional methods. Summative evaluation of such outcomes as critical thinking and therapeutic nursing interventions are required of programs seeking reaccreditation. A portfolio of student papers illustrating evidence of critical thinking or competencies for faculty and students documenting skill proficiency is one method of program evaluation. Activities that encourage students to evaluate their progress over the course of a program or semester provide rich data to both the students and the faculty. Program evaluation portfolios require the collaboration of students and faculty in collecting, selecting, and organizing the portfolio submissions. As these collaborations evolve, with reflection from students and faculty, formative evaluation occurs and instructional methods are reinforced, revised, or modified.

Limitations of portfolios as a means of assessing students and faculty were identified as lack of demonstrated validity and reliability, limited time for assembling the portfolio, limited time for review of the portfolio by the evaluator(s), and limited space for storage and retrieval. Karlowicz (2000) described a portfolio pilot program including samples of instruments.

Tracy and colleagues (2000) outlined a program of authentic assessment. The portfolio component of the program was broken into three categories: clinical, theory, and holistic. The clinical achievement portfolio (CAP) was described in this article with a table of required paperwork and a scoring rubric. The scoring rubric rated each of the five required achievement areas on a five-point scale. The five areas evaluated were critical thinking, problem-solving, decision-making, communication, and accountability. The students gained a holistic view of their personal and professional roles in society because the CAP required integration of theory and reflection on clinical experiences.

In adult degree programs the portfolio process has also been used effectively. The portfolio has been integral in the process of awarding college credit for prior learning experiences of registered nurses who are seeking a higher degree (Alexander, Craft, & Baldwin 2002; Lettus, Moessner, & Dooley 2001). Nurses are required to submit evidence of significant professional experiences, supported by theory and reflection on those experiences. If the portfolio is rigorously developed, college credit can be awarded for these experiences.

Portfolio Use in Professional Nursing

Professional portfolios are becoming more common in nursing. The literature suggests that with the variability of nursing roles, professional mobility, cross training, and the need to provide evidence of competence, the professional nursing portfolio is an excellent tool. The professional nursing portfolio is a mechanism for applying Schon's concepts (1983) of reflection-in-action and reflection-on-action. Reflection-in-action refers to complex situations with no right or wrong answers. The practitioner must use knowledge, skills, analysis, synthesis, and intuition to respond to these complex situations. Reflection-on-action refers to the impact that past actions can have on future decisions through reflection. The portfolio process allows a practitioner to provide evidence of these complex processes (Bell 2001).

Competence must be ensured in clinical settings. Jasper (2001) describes a professional portfolio process implemented by nurse managers through the United Kingdom Central Council for Nurses, Midwives, and Health Visitors (UKCC) to document and evaluate competence in nursing staff. The process includes self-verification, peer review, and supervisor review. It was noted in the article that although initial educational standards exist, standards of continued nursing competence have yet to be developed.

The professional portfolio, developed over time, provides an opportunity not only for external evaluation but also for self-reflection. Periodic review of one's portfolio would provide feedback on growth, goal achievement, career path, and competence. The professional portfolio is a showcase of background and expertise (Oermann 2002).

Meister and colleagues (2002) reviewed the literature on portfolios as used by professional nurses. The authors took a global perspective and related the use of professional portfolios to the Benner (1984) model of nursing development. Benner described nursing proficiency on a continuum from novice to expert. Suggested tables of contents for student and experienced nurse portfolios were included in the article. The suggested experienced nurse portfolio content elements are very similar to the Genetic Nurses Credentialing Commission (GNCC) portfolio requirements, including evidence of formal and continuing education, peer and supervisor reviews, knowledge of nursing and healthcare literature, and self-reflection.

Validity and Reliability Implications

Validity and reliability of the portfolio process arises from the inclusion of sufficient breadth, currency, and authenticity of individually reliable submissions (Wilkinson et al. 2002). The richness, creativity, and variety of the portfolio are the strengths of the portfolio process. If an individual only includes the required items and does not adequately reflect on the submissions and the process, then the portfolio has little value. Strong evidence and a descriptive, reflective narrative increase the validity of the portfolio evaluation. The evaluation is more valid because a more detailed and complete story is being told. A descriptive reflection provides insight into the thoughts and rationale during the creation of the portfolio. The use of preestablished standards, developed by the reviewer, for construction and audit of the portfolios enhances their validity and ability to be compared to accepted patterns of achievement in the profession and elsewhere. Likewise, use of panels of experts, educators, and other authorities as consultants on requirements, formats, and evaluation can increase the credibility and integrity of portfolios as an approach to documenting student and professional accomplishments.

The use of portfolios for professional evaluation has only been documented in the literature for the past 20 years. Because portfolio assessment is a relatively new method for assessment, consistency, validity, and normative data are limited. Concerns regarding the time (Madaus & Kellaghan 1993; Abruscato 1993) and subjectivity (Ediger 2000b; Johnson, McDaniel, & Willeke 2000; Parsons 1998) of portfolio assembly and review have been documented. The literature does not present a strong case either for or against the use of portfolios for evaluation. Advantages include personalization of work, the ability to reflect on growth, and the development of thinking skills. Disadvantages include the subjectivity and time involved with the portfolio process. No strong validity or reliability data were found in the literature to support or refute the use of portfolios for evaluation (Pitts et al. 2002). Historical and research evidence both for and against the use of portfolios was primarily anecdotal.

Ethical and Legal Implications

Also of concern are issues of professional accountability (Greco & Mahon 2003). The need to maintain confidentiality in the portfolio review process is an important factor in professional portfolios. The creator of the portfolio must protect the privacy and confidentiality of others referred to in the portfolio (Fitch 2001; Sheahan 2002). For example, when client case studies are required, the client information must be made anonymous. This alteration, however, becomes problematic when pedigrees (genograms) and other representations of family histories are necessary to describe, define, and contextualize the client situation.

Ethics are another consideration in the portfolio process (Hinderer & Hinderer 2001). The portfolio submissions must be accurate examples of the professional's performance. In reviewing a professional portfolio, the information provided must be able to be tracked and verified (Fitch 2001). A mechanism must be in place that validates the accuracy of the portfolio contents. Again, in the situation involving client information, an internal validation that will not jeopardize client confidentiality can be included in the portfolio, such as the verification of care provided completed by a peer or supervisor. The review of the portfolio can then evaluate the contents with the validation that the information is accurate. When portfolios are used as a tool to measure or ensure professional competence, the process needs to be clearly defined, psychometrically sound, and legally defensible (Whittaker, Carson, & Smolenski, 2000). Multiple reviewers with proven inter-rater reliability on audit tools provide valid and reliable results that are defensible. Faculties need to be able to substantiate a student's grade that is based on a portfolio review. Professional organizations must consider their reputation, legal liability, and advocacy for public welfare (Hamm 2000) when implementing the portfolio process. The decision to award or withhold a credential, degree, or passing grade based on portfolio review must be taken very seriously, and be based on specific, identified criteria. The decision process must be tracked and able to be replicated in order to hold up to the scrutiny of colleagues, supervisors, and the public. Legal consultation for review of the portfolio process is advisable to protect the applicants, the organization, and the reviewers.

Summary

The concept of portfolio and its use in professional education has developed and been refined over time through the process of trial and error. Although the concept of portfolio is used in a variety of settings, the review of literature yielded the common defining attributes of organized, individualized, selective, ongoing, and reflective, which could be applied to investment, creative, descriptive, and evaluative portfolios in professional and educational settings. As portfolios are becoming more common in a variety of settings, psychometric data on the validity and reliability of the requirements and the review process are needed to establish the strength of the portfolio approach to documenting professional achievements. In addition, psychometric examination is needed to establish the validity of the portfolio approach in depicting the creator's knowledge, abilities, attitudes, values, beliefs, and skills.

References

Abruscato, J. (1993, February). Early results and tentative implications from the Vermont portfolio project. *Phi Delta Kappan*, 474–477.

Alexander, J. G., Craft, S. W., & Baldwin, M. S. (2002). The nursing portfolio: A reflection of a professional. *Journal of Continuing Education in Nursing, 33*(2), 55–59.

Alschuler, A. S. (1996). The portfolio emperor has no clothes: He should stay naked. *Counselor Education & Supervision, 36*, 133+. Retrieved May 30, 2001, from EBSCOhost (Academic Search Elite), http://ehostvgw18.epnet.com.

Alsop, A. (2001). Competence unfurled: Developing portfolio practice. *Occupational Therapy International, 8*(2), 126–131.

Arter, J. A., Spandel, V., & Culham, R. (1995). *Portfolios for assessment and instruction* (Contract no. RR93002004). Washington, DC: Office of Educational Research and Improvement. (ERIC Document Reproduction Service no. EDO-CG-95-10)

Baltimore, M. L., & Hickson, J. (1996). Portfolio assessment: A model for counselor education. *Counselor Education & Supervision, 36*, 113+. Retrieved May 30, 2001, from EBSCOhost (Academic Search Elite), http://ehostvgw18.epnet.com.

Bell, S. K. (2001). Professional nurse's portfolio. *Nursing Administration Quarterly, 25*(2), 69–73.

Ben-David, M. F. (2000). The role of assessment in expanding professional horizons. *Medical Teacher, 22*(5), 472–477.

Benner, P. (1984). *From novice to expert: Excellence and power in clinical nursing practice.* Menlo Park, CA: Addison-Wesley.

Bernstein, D., & Edwards, R. (2001, January 5). We need objective, rigorous peer review of teaching. *Chronicle of Higher Education,* B24.

Bradley, A. (1994). Pioneers in professionalism. *Education Week, 13*(30), 18–25.

Bratt, M. M. (1998). Reflective journaling: Fostering learning in clinical experiences. *Dean's Notes, 20*(1), 1–3.

Brogan, B. R. (1995). What will outcome-based education mean for our children? *New Schools, New Communities, 11*(3), 13–18.

———. (1996, March 10). *Rethinking supervision and evaluation: Why one school district is using professional portfolios.* Paper presented at the 128th annual conference of the American Association of School Administrators, San Diego, CA.

Brookfield, S. D. (1995). *Becoming a critically reflective teacher.* San Francisco: Jossey-Bass.

Camp, R. (1998). Portfolio reflection: The basis for dialogue. *Clearing House, 72*(1), 10+. Retrieved May 30, 2001, from EBSCOhost (Academic Search Elite), http://ehostvgw18.epnet.com.

Campbell, D. (2000). Authentic assessment and authentic standards. *Phi Delta Kappan, 81*, 405–407.

Chambers, R. (2002, June 17). Adopt APD to make appraisal simpler. *General Practitioner*, 44.

Costanza, R., Daly, H., Folke, C., Hawken, P., Holling, C. S., & McMichael, A. J. (2000). Managing our environmental portfolio. *Bioscience, 50*, 149+. Retrieved May 30, 2001, from EBSCOhost (Academic Search Elite), http://ehostvgw18.epnet.com.

Darbyshire, P. (1995). Lessons for literature: Caring, interpretation, and dialogue. *Journal of Nursing Education, 34*, 211–216.

Davis, M. H., Ben-David, M. F., Harden, R. M., Ker, P.H.J., McGhee, C., Pippard, M. J., et al. (2001). Portfolio assessment in medical students' final examinations. *Medical Teacher, 23*(4), 357–366.

Donen, N. (1998). No to mandatory continuing medical education, yes to mandatory practice auditing and professional educational development. *Canadian Medical Association Journal, 158*(8), 1044–1046.

Doolittle, P. (1994). *Teacher portfolio assessment* (Contract no. RR93002002). Washington, DC: Office of Educational Research and Improvement. (ERIC Document Reproduction Service no. EDO-TM-94-07)

Dutt-Doner, K. M., & Gilman, D. A. (1998). Students react to portfolio assessment. *Contemporary Education, 69*, 159+. Retrieved May 24, 2001, from OCLC FirstSearch (WilsonSelectPlus_FT), http://newfirstsearch.oclc.org.

Dyne, P. L., Strauss, R. W., & Rinnert, S. (2002). Systems-based practice: The sixth core competency. *Academic Emergency Medicine: Official Journal of the Society for Academic Emergency Medicine, 9*, 1270–1277.

Ediger, M. (2000a). Portfolios, maps and globes in geography. *College Student Journal, 34*(1), 22+. Retrieved May 30, 2001, from EBSCOhost (Academic Search Elite), http://ehostvgw18.epnet.com.

———. (2000b). Portfolios: Will they endure? *College Student Journal, 34*(1), 38+. Retrieved May 30, 2001, from EBSCOhost (Academic Search Elite), http://ehostvgw18.epnet.com.

Eyler, J., Giles, D. E., Jr., & Schmiede, A. (1996). *A practitioner's guide to reflection in service-learning: Student voices & reflections.* Nashville: Vanderbilt University.

Fitch, K. A. (2001). Process. College of DuPage, Liberal Arts Division. Retrieved March 7, 2003, from the World Wide Web: http://www.kafkaz.net/webfolios/process.htm.

Foote, C. J., & Vermette, P. J. (2001). Teaching Portfolio 101: Implementing the teaching portfolio in introductory courses. *Journal of Instructional Psychology, 28*(1), 31+. Retrieved May 30, 2001, from EBSCOhost (Academic Search Elite), http://ehostvgw18.epnet.com.

Greco, K. E., & Mahon, S. M. (2003). Genetics nursing practice enters a new era with credentialing. *Internet Journal of Advanced Nursing Practice, 5*(2). Retrieved March 10, 2003, from the World Wide Web: http://www.ispub.com/ostia/index.pnp.xmlfilepath=journals/ijanp/vol5n2/genetics.xml.

Hamm, M. S. (2000). Establishing and demonstrating the value of a credential. In C. G. Schoon & I. L. Smith (Eds.), *The licensure and certification mission: Legal, social, and political foundations* (pp. 31–52). New York: Professional Examination Service.

Hebert, E. A. (1998). Lessons learned about student portfolios. *Phi Delta Kappan, 79*, 583+. Retrieved May 24, 2001, from OCLC FirstSearch (WilsonSelectPlus_FT), http://newfirstsearch.oclc.org.

Herman, J. L., & Winters, L. (1994, October). Portfolio research: A slim collection. *Educational Leadership*, 48–55.

Hewitt, G. (2001). The writing portfolio: Assessment starts with A. *Clearing House, 74*, 187+. Retrieved May 30, 2001, from EBSCOhost (Academic Search Elite), http://ehostvgw18.epnet.com.

Hinderer, D. E., & Hinderer, S. R. (2001). *A multidisciplinary approach to health care ethics*. Mountain View, CA: Mayfield.

Jasper, M. (2001). The role of the nurse manager in ensuring competence: The use of portfolios and reflective writing. *Journal of Nursing Management, 9*(5), 249–251.

Jensen, G. M., & Saylor, C. (1994). Portfolios and professional development in the health professions. *Evaluation & the Health Professions, 17*(3), 344–357.

Johnson, R. L., McDaniel, F., & Willeke, M. J. (2000). Using portfolios in program evaluation: An investigation of interrater reliability. *American Journal of Evaluation, 21*(1), 65+. Retrieved May 30, 2001, from EBSCOhost (Academic Search Elite), http://ehostvgw18.epnet.com.

Karlowicz, K. A. (2000). The value of student portfolios to evaluate undergraduate nursing programs. *Nurse Educator, 25*, 82–87.

LaBoskey, V. K. (2000). Portfolios here, portfolios there. . . . Searching for the essence of "educational portfolios." *Phi Delta Kappan, 81*, 590–595.

Lettus, M. K., Moessner, P. H., & Dooley, L. (2001). The clinical portfolio as an assessment tool. *Nursing Administration Quarterly, 25* (2), 74-79.

Lyons, N. P. (1996, March). A grassroots experiment in performance assessment. *Educational Leadership*, 64–67.

Madaus, G. F., & Kellaghan, T. (1993). The British experience with "authentic" testing. *Phi Delta Kappan, 74*, 458–469.

Magill, S. L., & Herden, R. P. (1998). Using educational outcomes and student portfolios to steer management education. *Journal of Management Education, 22*, 567+. Retrieved November 14, 2000, from EBSCOhost (Academic Search Elite), http://ehostvgw18.epnet.com.

Maich, N. M., Brown, B., & Royle, J. (2000). "Becoming" through reflection and professional portfolios: The voice of growth in nurses. *Reflective Practice, 1*(3), 309–324.

Meister, L., Heath, J., Andrews, J., & Tingen, M. S. (2002). Professional nursing portfolios: A global perspective. *MEDSURG Nursing, 11*(4), 177–182.

Melograno, V. J. (1994, October). Portfolio assessment: Documenting authentic student learning. *Journal of Physical Education, Recreation, and Dance*, 50–61.

Mills, E. (1997). Portfolios: A challenge for technology. *International Journal of Instructional Media, 24*(1), 23+. Retrieved May 30, 2001, from EBSCOhost (Academic Search Elite), http://ehostvgw18.epnet.com.

Oermann, M. H. (2002). Developing a professional portfolio in nursing. *Orthopaedic Nursing, 21*(2), 73–78.

Parsons, J. (1998). Portfolio assessment: Let us proceed with caution. *Adult Learning, 9*(4), 28+. Retrieved May 30, 2001, from EBSCOhost (Academic Search Elite), http://ehostvgw18.epnet.com.

Pitts, J., Coles, C., Thomas, P., & Smith, F. (2002). Enhancing reliability in portfolio assessment: Discussions between assessors. *Medical Teacher, 24*(2), 197–201.

Popham, W. J. (1993). Circumventing the high costs of authentic assessment. *Phi Delta Kappan, 74,* 470–473.

Robinson, D. (1998). Student portfolios in mathematics. *Mathematics Teacher, 91,* 318+. Retrieved May 30, 2001, from EBSCOhost (Academic Search Elite), http://ehostvgw18.epnet.com.

Routledge, J., & Willson, M. (1997). Reflection on the development of a reflective assessment. *Medical Teacher, 19,* 122+. Retrieved May 30, 2001, from EBSCOhost (Academic Search Elite), http://ehostvgw18.epnet.com.

Ryan, M., & Carlton, K. H. (1997). Portfolio application in a school of nursing. *Nurse Educator, 22*(1), 35–39.

Salend, S. J. (2001). Creating your own professional portfolio. *Intervention in School & Clinic, 36*(4), 195+. Retrieved May 30, 2001, from EBSCOhost (Academic Search Elite), http://ehostvgw18.epnet.com.

Schilling, K. M., & Schilling, K. L. (1993, March 24). Point of view. *Chronicle of Higher Education,* A40.

Schon, D. A. (1983). *The reflective practitioner.* New York: Basic Books.

Senne, T. A., & Rikard, G. L. (2002). Experiencing the portfolio process during the internship: A comparative analysis of two PETE portfolio models. *Journal of Teaching in Physical Education, 21,* 309–336.

Serembus, J. F. (2000). Teaching the process of developing a professional portfolio. *Nurse Educator, 25*(6), 282–287.

Sheahan, E. (Ed.). (2002). *HIPAA training handbook for the nursing/clinical staff: An introduction to confidentiality and privacy under HIPAA.* Marblehead, MA: HCPro.

Shepard, L. (1989). Why we need better assessments. *Educational Leadership, 4,* 4–9.

Smith, K., & Tillema, H. (2001). Long-term influences of portfolios on professional development. *Scandinavian Journal of Educational Research, 45*(2), 183–203.

Snadden, D., & Thomas, M. (1998). The use of portfolio learning in medical education. *Medical Teacher, 20*(3), 192+. Retrieved November 14, 2000, from EBSCOhost (Academic Search Elite), http://ehostvgw18.epnet.com.

Sorrell, J. M., Brown, H. N., Silva, M. C., & Kohlenberg, E. M. (1997). Use of writing portfolios for interdisciplinary assessment of critical thinking outcomes of nursing students. *Nursing Forum, 32*(4), 12–24.

Taylor, I., Thomas, J., & Sage, H. (1999). Portfolios for learning and assessment: Laying the foundations for continuing professional development. *Social Work Education, 18*(2), 147–160.

Tierney, R. J., Clark, C., Fenner, L., Herter, R. J., Simpson, C. S., & Wiser, B. (1998). Portfolios: Assumptions, tensions, and possibilities. *Reading Research Quarterly, 33,* 474–486.

Tracy, S. M., Marino, G. J., Richo, K. M., & Daly, E. M. (2000). The clinical achievement portfolio: An outcomes-based assessment project in nursing education. *Nurse Educator, 25,* 241–246.

Webb, C., Bridacott, R., Gray, M., Jasper, M., Miller, C., & McMullan, M. (2002). *Medical Education, 36,* 897–898.

Weddle, D. O., Himburg, S. P., Collins, N., & Lewis, R. (2002). The professional development portfolio process: Setting goals for credentialing. *Journal of the American Dietetic Association, 120,* 1439–1444.

Wenzel, L. S., Briggs, K. L., & Puryear, B. L. (1998). Portfolio: Authentic assessment in the age of the curriculum revolution. *Journal of Nursing Education, 37,* 208–212.

Whittaker, S., Carson, W., & Smolenski, M. C. (2000, June 30). Assuring continued competence—policy questions and approaches: How should the profession respond? *Online Journal of Issues in Nursing.* Retrieved March 17, 2003, from the World Wide Web: http://nursingworld.org/ojin/topic10/tpc10_4.htm.

Wilkinson, T. J., Challis, M., Hobma, S. O., Newble, D. I., Parboosingh, J. T., & Sibbald, R. G. (2002). The use of portfolios for assessment of the competence and performance of doctors in practice. *Medical Education, 36*(10), 918–924.

Wilson, N. (1998). Educational standards and the problem of error. *Educational Policy Analysis Archive, 6*(10). Retrieved November 7, 2002, from the World Wide Web: http://olam.ed.asu.edu/epaa/v6n10/c18.htm.

Wolf, D. P. (1989, April). Portfolio assessment: Sampling student work. *Educational Leadership,* 35–39.

Woodward, H. (1998). Reflective journals and portfolios: Learning through assessment. *Assessment & Evaluation in Higher Education, 23,* 415–423.

Worthen, B. R. (1993). Is your school ready for alternative assessment? *Phi Delta Kappan, 74,* 455–456.

Portfolios: Current Uses 3

Robin Donohoe Dennison, RN, MSN, CCNS

While initial nursing competence is acquired through basic nursing education, competence in dynamic and lifelong learning is essential to meet the public's expectation of safe and effective care. Duyff defines lifelong learning as "a process that stimulates and empowers people to acquire knowledge, values, skills, and understanding that are needed in life" (2000, p. 538). Lifelong learning is then seen as a supportive process to stimulate and empower (Commission for a Nation of Lifelong Learning 1997). Since the individual is most aware of what skills and knowledge one needs to maintain competence in one's selected field, self-assessment of learning needs, establishment of personal goals, and seeking of learning experiences to meet the needs and achieve the goals are integral to lifelong learning. The process of lifelong learning includes personal reflection, establishment of short-term and long-term goals, assessment of knowledge and skills, development of a plan to reach the goals, implementation of the plan, and evaluation and refocusing of the plan (Duyff 2000).

The National Council of State Boards of Nursing (NCSBN) (1996) believes that standards of competence must be applicable to all nurses in all practice roles and should address the range of practitioner experience. Several methods of assessment and validation of continued competence have been proposed, including written re-examination, professional certification, peer review, case reviews, practice evaluations, computer simulations and virtual reality testing, targeted continuing education with outcomes measurement, employer skills testing, and professional portfolios (American Nurses Association [ANA] 1999; NCSBN 1996). While mandatory continuing education is used in many states for relicensure as a primary method of ensuring continued competence, continuing education programs document only attendance rather than demonstration and testing of continued competence. Also, there has been a lack of evidence of a correlation between participation in continuing education activities and improved practice (ANA 1999; Pearson 1998).

One process advocated as a method of validating continued competence is portfolio development and evaluation. Though interest in the use of portfolios has grown in the past few years in the United States, portfolios have been an integral part of preregistration education for decades in the United Kingdom and are now required for postregistration documentation of continued competence in the United Kingdom.

Oermann (2002) describes two types of portfolios: growth and development portfolios and best-work portfolios. A *growth and development portfolio* is intended to aid the nurse in monitoring progress toward personal and professional learning goals. It is a working document providing ongoing evidence of competencies and is not intended to be reviewed by others. Selected materials from the growth and development portfolio are included in a *best-work portfolio* to be reviewed by others for a specific purpose. A best-work portfolio provides evidence of the competencies of the nurse, to be used in situations in which other people will be reviewing the portfolio. Examples of such situations include applications for jobs, promotions, or postgraduate education, annual performance reviews, credentialing, certification, recertification, and reregistration. This type of portfolio contains selected material organized for review by others.

There is confusion regarding the terms "portfolio" and "profile." While the term "portfolio" may be defined as a broad compilation of "skills, knowledge, attitudes, understanding, and achievement," a profile is evidence selected from a personal portfolio for a specific purpose and the attention of a specific audience (Brown 1995), such as evidence Oermann (2002) described as being part of a *best-work portfolio*. This chapter will provide an overview of the use of portfolios and profiles in the health professions, education, and related fields.

Uses of Portfolios

Portfolios began to be used in nursing schools in the early 1980s (Budnick & Beaver 1984). Many articles have advocated the use of portfolios as part of the learning and evaluation process for undergraduate and graduate students (Alexander et al. 2002; Ball, Daly, & Carnwell 2000; DeNatale & Romeo 2000; Erickson, Niess, & Geller 2000; Forker & McDonald 1996; Gadbury-Amyot et al. 2000; Hayes et al. 2002; Karlowicz 2000; Ryan & Carlton 1997; Thomas, Lamson, & King 2001). Use of portfolios in this context allows the student to document his or her professional growth and learning related to the course objectives and allows the teacher to evaluate achievement of course objectives through this documentation. Portfolios may also be used to award credit for prior learning (Ryan & Carlton 1997).

In the 1990s, the portfolio emerged as a means of "transforming the nurse's experience into tangible vignettes where learning experiences could be identified as a building block of lifelong learning and reflected upon" (Ball, Daly, & Carnwell 2000, p. 35). The nurse would briefly describe a clinical situation such as administering a medication to the wrong patient and reflect upon what was learned from that experience. The expectation was that the portfolio would enable the nurse to plan learning so that it relates to his or her practice and choose relevant learning activities (Redfern & Hull 1997). Many articles have also advocated the use of portfolios for professional growth and career development (Bell 2001; Bradley 2001; Brooks, Barrett, & Zimmermann 1998; Brooks & Madda 1999; Campbell & Mackay 2001; Cayne 1995; Day 1998; Gellman 1993; Jasper 1995, 2001; Johnson 2002; Lettus, Harmon, & Dooley 2001; Melland & Volden 1996; Monsen et al. 2002). In this context, the nurse identifies short-term and long-term career goals, and professional activities and learning experiences are viewed in relationship to achieving these goals.

Cayne (1995) found that the process of portfolio preparation in itself encourages professional development by stimulating reflection on experience. This article described an action research project that explored whether the process of portfolio preparation does in fact encourage professional development and what influenced this process. Despite a small study group, Cayne concluded that the most valuable aspect of portfolios is the emphasis on experience as a means of learning and that the process of portfolio preparation may assist nurses to appreciate their experience as learning.

Examples of Uses of Portfolios in Nursing

United States

The Oklahoma Board of Nursing appointed a task force to conduct a statewide study to investigate the challenge of ensuring continued competence in 1997. The task force identified standards of nursing competency and proposed that nurses provide evidence that they met these standards in a "Professional Practice Profile" (PPP). The Oklahoma Board of Nursing developed a detailed portfolio format and scoring mechanism and conducted a pilot study to determine the score of the random sample in the late 1990s. The PPP was to include the nurse's résumé, evidence of formal and informal education or training, practice activities, professional activities, and volunteer activities, a summary including a self-assessment of strengths and weaknesses along with opportunities for improvement, and a brief statement identifying difficulties encountered in preparing the PPP.

Besides validating the competency of the nurse against the standards, the profile was to identify learning activities that would contribute to the nurse's continued competence in their practice setting. The task force developed a scoring system for use in a pilot study, which was conducted in 1998 using 90 registered nurses and 42 licensed practical nurses. A mean score was established for this pilot group, and the task force recommended a second pilot study to further evaluate weighting of the components and establishment of a passing score. However, at this point, the board voted to discontinue work on the development of the Professional Practice Profile, primarily based on concerns regarding cost and legal ramifications for the Oklahoma Board of Nursing. An analysis using the data from the pilot study revealed that the cost of using the PPP as a measure of continued competence at the time of licensure renewal would be significant, even if only a random sample of nurses were required to submit their profiles. The evaluation of the profiles would result in significant costs to the board associated with the need for additional staff members, office space, and storage space for profiles submitted and higher licensure fees, which are the primary source of the board's funding. Second, the board was concerned about the legal ramifications of nurses identifying their own strengths and weaknesses in a potentially discoverable document (G. McNish, personal communication, May 22, 2002, July 20, 2004).

The Kentucky Board of Nursing adopted a working position statement in 1997 that articulated the nurse's responsibility and accountability to demonstrate competency in the nurse's given practice role. Though the state had required 30 contact hours of continuing education credit every two years for relicensure for over 20 years, the board proposed the development of a professional portfolio to validate continued competence. Open forums were held across Kentucky in 1997 and early 1998 to explore the continued competence issues with representative nurses (McGuire & Weisenbeck 2001). Though the concept of a "portfolio" was eliminated from the proposed changes to the Kentucky nursing laws presented to the 2000 Kentucky General Assembly, nurses were given a choice of new competency validation mechanisms. The nurse may (1) continue to earn 30 contact hours of approved continuing education during the two-year relicensure period, (2) maintain national certification related to the nurse's practice role, or (3) earn 15 contact hours of continuing education during the two-year relicensure period along with conducting a nursing research project, publishing a nursing-related article, presenting a professional presentation, providing a satisfactory nursing employment evaluation, or providing a completed employer's skills checklist (S. Weisenbeck, personal communication, April 22, 2003).

The American Association of Critical-Care Nurses (2003) has also adopted a menu approach to renewing certification. Initial certification still requires a passing scoring on a multiple-choice examination, but recertification points can be obtained through a number of professional activities. The nurse must obtain 100 continuing education recognition points (CERPs) during the three-year period prior to the certification examination date, but the points can be earned through (1) attending continuing education programs, (2) earning academic course credit, (3) authoring, coauthoring, or editing professional nursing publications, (4) making professional presentations, (5) participating in activities to improve care in the clinical setting, (6) maintaining membership in a professional healthcare organization, (7) participating in volunteer activities, and (8) program development and/or leadership activities. Each contact hour of continuing education credit is equivalent to one CERP and the other activities are assigned point values.

The Genetic Nursing Credentialing Commission (GNCC), the credentialing commission of the International Society of Nurses in Genetics (ISONG), has used portfolios for awarding the Advanced Practice Nurse in Genetics (APNG) and the Genetics

Clinical Nurse (GCN) credential (R. Monsen, personal communication, May 21, 2002). To date, this is the only specialty certification that does not require initial examination. A score team of five raters evaluate each portfolio according to the GNCC standards for clinical practice. A computer software program referred to as Neural Net is used to ensure integrity of the scores and evaluate inter-rater reliability. The candidate is assigned a "met" or "not met" final score, considering the scores by all raters (Monsen et al. 2002). The Genetic Nursing Credentialing Commission has used portfolio evaluation to certify 17 APNGs and 3 GCNs, and considers its experience with using portfolios for certification to be successful because it is rigorous and cost-effective and has gained the respect of other genetics healthcare providers (R. Monsen, personal communication, May 28, 2003). It has also been accepted by genetics nurse clinicians.

The National Association of Clinical Nurse Specialists (NACNS) included a professional portfolio option for certification in its strategic plan during its annual meeting in 2003 (C. Filipovich, personal communication, May 21, 2003). The plan includes the use of a "core" CNS certification examination that would test for core CNS competencies as delineated in the NACNS *Statement on Clinical Nurse Specialist Practice and Education*, along with an evaluation of specialty practice. This evaluation of specialty practice would be a specialty examination when available for the CNS's specialty or a portfolio submission and evaluation for the specialty component if a specialty examination is not available (Lyon 2002). Lyon and Boland (2002) believe that the flexibility of the portfolio approach is particularly helpful in evaluating new or evolving CNS specialty areas and that it is especially attractive for specialty areas where no CNS examination is available. Though the specific components of the portfolio have not been finalized, reflective learning and peer review along with linking outcome data to job performance in each sphere of influence pertinent to a particular CNS's scope of practice have been recommended (Lyon & Boland 2002).

United Kingdom

Postregistration Education and Practice (PREP)

In November 2001, the Department of Health of the United Kingdom published *Working Together, Learning Together* as a framework for lifelong learning for the National Health Service. Lifelong learning was described as being primarily about growth and opportunity along with ensuring that staff are supported in the acquisition of new skills and the realization of their potential. The belief that learning should be valued, recognized, recorded, and accredited whenever possible was confirmed in this report. The framework strengthens the links between continuing professional development and revalidation and reregistration of professional staff (Department of Health of United Kingdom 2001). Personal development plans are also part of the lifelong learning framework. The plans are to include objectives for the short-, medium-, and long-term criteria for measuring whether the employee has achieved his or her objectives, an action plan for how the objectives will be achieved, and dates

FIGURE 3-1 Process for the Development of a Personal Development Plan

Source: Reprinted with permission.

for evaluation and review (Leifer 2002). The process for development of a personal development plan is illustrated in Figure 3-1.

The first step is review, which is intended to assess the current knowledge and skills and strengths and weaknesses. The next step is planning and action, which includes the establishment of a plan for meeting learning needs and engaging in a learning activity to meet those needs. The final step is recording the plan and the learning activity and reflecting on the learning experience after completion to consider whether the activity met the needs (Royal College of Nursing [RCN] 2003a).

The Nursing and Midwifery Council (NMC) (previously referred to as the United Kingdom Central Council for Nurses, Midwives and Health Visitors [UKCC]) has issued a set of standards referred to as the postregistration education and practice (PREP) standards (UKCC 1994). These standards specify the minimum elements required to maintain registration as a nurse, midwife, or health visitor. The PREP guidelines focus on the development of individual nurses, midwives, and health visitors in order to maintain and improve standards of patient and client care. The guidelines acknowledge that the knowledge and competence achieved at the point of registration need to be maintained and improved in order to promote higher standards of practice. One of the elements required to continue registration is the maintenance of a "Personal Professional Profile" (PPP). Brown (1995) defines a profile as a collection of evidence that is selected from a professional portfolio for a specific purpose and audience, which is similar to Oermann's definition (2002) of a best-work portfolio. This PPP is to provide evidence of each nurse's continuing professional development, demonstrating the knowledge and competence that improves standards of practice. The PPP is used by the NMC as evidence that each nurse has attained the standards for education and practice required under the auspices of PREP. It is used for periodic registration verifying continuous nursing practice and to provide a record of learning and confirmation of professional development (Jasper 1995). The PPP is a summary of the current three years of practice, which can be added to a more comprehensive professional portfolio, and is the central method of demonstrating fitness to practice and remain registered (Neades 2003).

The NMC believes that a PPP that is relevant to the individual and the employer along with a good appraisal makes more sense than just five study days over three years. Though the NMC never actually asks to see a portfolio or even a profile, the nurse must extract information from the profile as evidence of continuing learning. (T. Milam, personal communication, March 17, 2003). The NMC (2002) described its procedures to audit compliance with the PREP standards. A sample of registrants are asked to provide the NMC with a description of their learning activities and the relevance of the learning to their work. If asked to take part in the audit, a nurse needs to provide evidence, using PREP summary forms provided by the NMC.

Even though a PPP is required to continue registration, evidence indicates that many nurses either do not have a PPP or do not make entries to their PPP on a regular basis. Richardson (1998) conducted a descriptive study to evaluate the use of personal professional profiles, and wrote that profile development encourages active participation in learning and facilitates continuing education. A questionnaire was distributed to a stratified random sampling taken from all grades of nurses, midwives, and health visitors in a United Kingdom trust, and 121 of 194 were completed and returned. Nineteen percent did not have a profile, and of the 98 that did have a profile, 56% made irregular reflective entries and 32% had either not made any entry or only placed certificates in the profile. Sixty-four percent of the 98 that did have a profile said that they used reflective practice but did not record self-reflection in their profile. Eighty-three percent felt that profiling was time-consuming. Sixty-six percent of the 98 subjects that did have a profile reported that the profile had many benefits, such as helping the nurse to focus on clinical practice, but most felt that they had insufficient encouragement and advice on profile development from nursing leadership. This study supports the benefits of portfolios as a learning tool and emphasizes the need for an efficient approach. This study supports the inclusion of self-reflection, though Richardson stated that more evidence was needed to support the hypothesis that reflective practice leads to improved outcomes. Andrews, Gidman, and Humphreys (1998) state that there is scant empirical evidence to suggest that improved patient care takes place as a direct result of reflection, but the United Kingdom Nurse Midwifery Council expects all nurses to engage in some form of reflective activity and to include written entries in the PPP.

E-Portfolio

The Royal College of Nursing (RCN) in the United Kingdom offers members an opportunity to develop their portfolio electronically (Layte & Ravet 2003). An electronic or digital portfolio is similar to a traditional portfolio except that it is stored, maintained, and shared electronically, which allows for easy distribution and revision (Lammintakanen et al. 2002). The RCN version is referred to as an e-portfolio. It is accessed through the RCN members-only Learning Zone web site. The RCN Learning Zone offers its members a number of services, including online full-text journals, meeting places, clinical guidelines, bite-size chunks of learning, career information, and an electronic portfolio. The e-portfolio is the most frequently accessed area of the Learning Zone (M. Semple, personal communication, March 19, 2003).

The e-portfolio contains professional details and action plans, along with evidence of learning and professional practice. Users are encouraged to consider the widest range of learning activities, so in addition to formal and certificated educational events, prompts are offered to consider learning from a range of informal learning activities including direct care. The portfolio enables material to be e-mailed directly to colleagues or supervisors and can be used to automatically generate curriculum vitae. It could also be used for professional accreditation and academic awards, offering the possibility of developing profiles for specific purposes. Nurses may choose the format for printing the portfolio, including a format appropriate for the Nursing and Midwifery Council's PREP requirements (M. Semple, personal communication, March 19, 2003). The easy access for members allows the nurse to enter everyday learning experiences and appropriate reflection at the time of occurrence rather than trying to reproduce the information from memory at the time of re-registration. While the Learning Zone's immediate aim is to promote flexible lifelong learning and support nurses' professional development, the RCN firmly believes that it will also have a powerful impact on patient care (M. Semple, personal communication, June 5, 2003).

Faculty of Emergency Nursing

The newly developed Faculty of Emergency Nursing (FEN) in the United Kingdom utilizes portfolio evaluation against clearly defined levels of competency. The Royal College of Nursing and the RCN Accident and Emergency Association initiated the faculty concept in 1997. The FEN was formally launched at the RCN Congress in April 2003 (L. McBride, personal communication, May 22, 2003). The Faculty of Emergency Nursing is a professional nursing body intended to "develop and maintain high standards of competence and professional integrity and facilitate leadership" within the specialty of emergency nursing. The FEN has defined standards of competence for emergency nurses, will provide leadership within the specialty of emergency nursing, and will focus on continuing professional development of emergency nurses. The faculty enables nurses to progress through a defined career and competency framework and the maintenance of standards of practice. Nurses have an opportunity to perform a self-assessment to determine whether they should apply to become an associate, a member, or a fellow of the faculty. These are the three career benchmarks described by the faculty, and standards of competence have been developed for each of these benchmarks. Core and specialist competencies in eight areas of emergency practice have been defined for each of these levels (Windle, 2003). These eight areas include prehospital care, major incident planning, care of the patient with psychological needs, major trauma management, emergency care of the person with minor injury or illness, and emergency care of the child and younger person (RCN 2003b).

Admission to the Faculty of Emergency Nursing depends on a peer review process. In the founding period (first two years) applicants must demonstrate evidence of achievement in practice against clearly defined competency standards within a career framework through self-assessment, complete curriculum vitae, and a peer review statement. In the postfounding period applicants must demonstrate evidence of achievement in practice through presentation of a portfolio to a FEN peer review panel. The portfolio is evaluated to determine achievement of the standards of competence for emergency nurses. Successful applicants in the founding and postfounding period will receive RCN accreditation of their professional practice (L. McBride, personal communication, May 22, 2003).

Canada

The College of Nurses of Ontario (CNO) has addressed the issue of continued competence and competence evaluation through three areas of focus: reflective practice, practice review, and a Practice Setting Consultation Project.

Reflective Practice

The first component is a self-directed reflective practice process to help the nurse to continually improve his or her practice. All nurses are responsible for participating in a reflective practice exercise annually by completing a self-assessment, obtaining peer feedback, creating a learning plan, implementing the learning plan, and evaluating the learning. The nurse may choose any one of five options to meet the reflective practice requirements. These options are a Self-Assessment Tool, which is available on the Internet, an employer's professional development system, a professional profile, formal focused learning, or a personally designed system that includes self-assessment, peer feedback, and development of a learning plan. The professional profile described here includes a comprehensive self-assessment, résumé information, prior learning assessments, and plans for learning. A Do-It-Yourself Guide to Reflective Practice is available by the Internet to assist nurses in learning more about the concepts and purposes of reflective practice (College of Nurses of Ontario Quality Assurance Program 1999).

Practice Review

The second component is a practice review, focusing on facilitation of practice areas identified for improvement. Nurses are randomly selected to participate in this practice assessment component, followed by education and remediation according to identified weaknesses (Campbell & Mackay 2001). One hundred nurses were selected and tested using a written assessment tool during the first evaluation cycle. From this initial sample, 94 nurses successfully completed the written assessment and 6 nurses were identified as requiring an additional assessment using a behavior-based interview conducted by a Practice Consultant at the College of Nurses. Following the assessments, reports were provided to the Quality Assessment Committee, which subsequently made decisions about remedial activities for these nurses, and the college worked with these nurses to facilitate their learning activities (B. Campbell, personal communication, June 3, 2003).

Consultation Project

The final component is the Practice Setting Consultation Project, designed to assist employers to foster organizational characteristics that promote quality professional practice (Campbell & Mackay 2001). The College of Nurses of Ontario has developed a model, referred to as the Quality Practice Setting Attributes Model, which identified the seven key system attributes that support professional practice: care delivery process, communication systems, equipment and facilities, leadership, organizational supports, professional development systems, and response systems to external demands (Campbell & Mackay 2001). This model is well respected by nurse clinicians, employers, and the Canadian healthcare system.

Australia

In Australia the registration of nurses is the responsibility of each state and territory. Nurses in each state must declare competence on renewal of license in order to maintain registration. Several states have implemented an audit system, which others are following, that requires a nurse to provide evidence of competence. A professional portfolio is suggested as one way of providing this evidence, but it is not mandatory at this time (J. Fletcher, personal communication, May 22, 2003).

Examples of Uses of Portfolios in Other Professions

Dietetics

The Commission on Dietetic Registration (CDR) and the American Dietetic Association (ADA) have implemented a major change from the previous process of mandatory reporting of continuing education hours to their new recertification process utilizing the Professional Development Portfolio (PDP). This change was implemented in June 2001 and will be phased in from 2001 to 2005. The PDP includes:

- professional self-reflection
- learning needs assessment

- learning plan development
- implementation of learning plan through continuing professional education (CPE)
- evaluation of learning plan outcomes

Worksheets are available on the Internet to aid dieticians in this five-step process. Submission of the learning activities log is required. Continuing education hours are still required as part of fulfillment of the learning plan, and each continuing education activity must relate to a learning need identified on the learning plan (Keim, Johnson, & Gates 2001).

The ADA's credentialing program also uses a portfolio-based assessment. Three of the components of the portfolio—education, practice experience, and professional achievement—require documentation that established criteria for the components have been met. Two other components—professional roles and colleagues—use a self-report format. The final component—approach to practice—is measured by a structured written response to a hypothetical practice situation (Bradley 1996).

Occupational Therapy

The Professional Development Tool (PDT) of the American Occupational Therapy Association (AOTA), developed as part of the association's Continuing Competence Plan for Professional Development, contains three primary elements: self-assessment tools, guidelines for establishing a professional development plan, and a suggested framework and guidelines for a professional portfolio (Hull & Smith 2002). The Professional Development Tool is available through the association's web site to assist members in assessing their learning needs, developing a learning plan, selecting resources to meet the specific learning goals, documenting progress toward the learning goals, and reflecting on how the learning has improved their personal practice. The PDT also suggests a portfolio format for documenting their accomplishments and professional activities (AOTA 2003). AOTA members are encouraged to maintain a current portfolio. Portfolio evaluation is expected to be used as the process by which Specialty Certification and Board Certification are awarded. The specific requirements for both of these certifications are not yet finalized (S. Hertfelder, personal communication, June 13, 2003).

Medicine

Portfolio-based recertification is one of the options in a menu of choices for recertification in general practice of medicine in the United Kingdom. There, Snadden and Thomas (1998) describe the use of portfolios in medicine as a method of tracking personal development, as a formative learning tool, and as a summative assessment tool. They recommend inclusion of critical incidents of events with patients, a reflective diary, clinical experiences, projects, critical reviews of articles, feedback from mentors or supervisors, and video recordings of consultations. In the United States, applications for hospital privileges frequently resemble a portfolio as a collection of achievements; but portfolios, as such, are not a current requirement for continuing licensure in medicine.

Education

Wolf defines a teaching portfolio as a "collection of information about a teacher's practice" (1996, p. 34). It can include such evidence as lesson plans, student assignments, written descriptions or videotapes of the teacher's instruction, anecdotal records made by the teacher, letters of recommendation, and formal evaluations by supervisors and student.

Teachers frequently use a professional portfolio as part of their hiring, retention, evaluation, and promotion process (Salend 2001). The National Board for Professional Teaching Standards (NBPTS) offers National Board Certification (NBC). Candidates participate in assessments based on National Board standards for accomplished teaching. All assessments consist of a portfolio and performance at an assessment center. The portfolio includes classroom artifacts such as videotapes or samples of student works and evidence of work within the profession and with families and the community. The Assessment Center consists of six 30-minute computer-delivered exercises (National Education Association 2001).

Summary

The use of portfolios for documentation of competency and continued competence is expanding in nursing and other professions. The portfolio provides documentation of active professional practice and participation in professional activities. To provide a format for lifelong learning, the portfolio should also include a self-assessment, identification of learning needs, a plan for meeting those needs, and documentation of implementation of the plan. Education is needed regarding the purpose and use of portfolios and the process of developing a portfolio and a professional development plan for continued competence.

References

Alexander, J. G., Craft, S. W., Baldwin, M. S., Beers, G. W., & McDaniel, G. S. (2002). The nursing portfolio: A reflection of a professional. *Journal of Continuing Education in Nursing, 33*(2), 55–59.

American Association of Critical-Care Nurses. (2003). *CCRN Certification Handbook*. Retrieved May 26, 2003, from http://www.certcorp.org/certcorp/certcorp.nsf/edcfc72ba47aaa708825666b0064bdcf/2117e64b8102b269882566710076d5ad?opendocument.

American Nurses Association (ANA). (1999). *Continued Competence.* Washington, DC: ANA.

American Occupational Therapy Association (AOTA). (2003). *Welcome to the PDT.* Retrieved June 12, 2003, from http://www.aota.org/pdt.

Andrews, M., Gidman, J., & Humphreys, A. (1998). Reflection: Does it enhance professional nursing practice? *British Journal of Nursing, 7,* 413–417.

Ball, E., Daly, W. M., & Carnwell, R. (2000). The use of portfolios in the assessment of learning and competence. *Nursing Standard, 14*(43), 35–37.

Bell, S. K. (2001). Professional nurse's portfolio. *Nursing Administration Quarterly, 25*(2), 69–73.

Bradley, C. A. (2001). Your role in your annual performance evaluation. *American Journal of Nursing, 101*(7), 71–74.

Bradley, R. (1996). Fellow of the American Dietetic Association credentialing program: Development and implementation of a portfolio-based assessment. *Journal of the American Dietetic Association, 96*(5), 513–517.

Brooks, B., Barrett, S., & Zimmermann, P. G. (1998). Beyond your resume: A nurse's professional "portfolio." *Journal of Emergency Nursing, 24*(6), 555–557.

Brooks, B., & Madda, M. (1999). How to organize a professional portfolio for staff and career development. *Journal for Nurses in Staff Development, 15*(1), 5–10.

Brown, R. A. (1995). *Portfolio development and profiling for nurses.* 2nd ed. Salisbury, Wilts: Quay Books.

Budnick, D., & Beaver, S. (1984). A student perspective on the portfolio. *Nursing Outlook, 32*(5), 268–270.

Campbell, B., & Mackay, G. (2001). Continuing competence: An Ontario nursing regulatory program that supports nurses and employers. *Nursing Administration Quarterly, 25*(2), 22–30.

Cayne, J. V. (1995). Portfolios: A developmental influence? *Journal of Advanced Nursing, 21*(2), 395–405.

College of Nurses of Ontario Quality Assurance Program. (1999). *Spotlight on reflective practice.* Retrieved May 25, 2003, from http://www.cno.org/qa/qa_refprac.html.

Commission for a Nation of Lifelong Learning. (1997). *A national learning: Vision for the 21st century.* Washington, DC: Commission for a Nation of Lifelong Learning.

Day, M. (1998). Community education: A portfolio approach. *Nursing Standard, 13*(10), 40–44.

DeNatale, M. L., & Romeo, R. (2000). Portfolios: Documenting learning in a personal way. *Nurse Educator, 25*(2), 69, 75.

Department of Health of United Kingdom. (2001). *Working together—learning together: A framework for lifelong learning for the NHS.* London: Department of Health.

Duyff, R. (2000). The value of lifelong learning: Key element in professional career development. *Journal of the American Dietetic Association, 99*(5), 538–544.

Erickson, D., Niess, M., & Geller, M. (2000, February 10–12). *Formative and summative portfolio assessment in a preservice secondary mathematics teacher education program.* Paper presented at the annual meeting of the Association for Mathematics Teacher Education, Charlotte, NC.

Forker, J. E., & McDonald, M. E. (1996). Methodological trends in healthcare professionals: Portfolio assessment. *Nurse Educator, 21*(5), 9–10.

Gadbury-Amyot, C., Holt, L., Overman, P., & Schmidt, C. (2000). Implementation of portfolio assessment in a competency-based dental hygiene program. *Journal of Dental Education, 64*(5), 375–380.

Gellman, E. (1993). The use of portfolios in assessing teacher competence: Measurement issues. *Action in Teacher Education, 14*(4), 39–44.

Hayes, E., Chandler, G., Merriam, D., & King, M. C. (2002). The master's portfolio: Validating a career in advanced practice nursing. *Journal of the American Academy of Nursing Practitioners, 14*(3), 119–125.

Hull, A., & Smith, K. C. (2002). *Continuing competence update.* Retrieved May 10, 2002, from http://www.aota.org/featured/area2/links16dd.asp.

Jasper, M. (1995). The potential of the professional portfolio in nursing. *Journal of Clinical Nursing, 4*(4), 249–255.

———. (2001). The role of the nurse manager in ensuring competence. The use of portfolios and reflective writing. *Journal of Nursing Management, 9*, 249–251.

Johnson, S. (2002). Development of educator competencies and the professional review process. *Journal for Nurses in Staff Development, 18*(2), 92–102.

Karlowicz, K. A. (2000). The value of student portfolios to evaluate undergraduate nursing programs. *Nurse Educator, 25*(2), 82–87.

Keim, K., Johnson, C., & Gates, G. (2001). Learning needs and continuing professional education activities of Professional Development Portfolio participants. *Journal of the American Dietetic Association, 101*(6), 697–702.

Lammintakanen, J., Saranto, K., Kivinen, T., & Kinnunen, J. (2002). The digital portfolio: A tool for human resource management in health care? *Journal of Nursing Management, 10*, 321–328.

Layte, M., & Ravet, S. (2003). The e-portfolio—case study: The Royal College of Nursing. *Learning in a Knowledge Europe Newsletter, 1*(1), 3–6.

Leifer, D. (2002). Do you have a plan? *Nursing Standard, 16*(41), 14–17.

Lettus, M. K., Harmon, P., & Dooley, L. (2001). The clinical portfolio as an assessment tool. *Nursing Administration Quarterly, 25*(2), 74–79.

Lyon, B. L. (2002). The regulation of clinical nurse specialist practice: Issues and current development. *Clinical Nurse Specialist, 16*(5), 239–241.

Lyon, B. L., & Boland, D. L. (2002). Demonstration of continued competence: A complex challenge. *Clinical Nurse Specialist, 16*(3), 155–156.

McGuire, C., & Weisenbeck, S. (2001). Revolution or evolution: Competency validation in Kentucky. *Nursing Administration Quarterly, 25*(2), 31–37.

Melland, H., & Volden, C. (1996). Teaching portfolios for faculty evaluation. *Nurse Educator, 21*(2), 35–38.

Monsen, R. B., Cook, S. S., Middelton, L., & Kase, R. (2002, January 31–February 1). *The Advanced Practice Nurse in Genetics Credential: Portfolio evaluation via Neural Net.* Paper presented at the National Coalition for Health Professional Education in Genetics, Bethesda, MD.

National Council of State Boards of Nursing (NCSBN). (1996). *Assuring competence.* Retrieved May 20, 2002, from http://www.ncsbn.org/public/resources/ncsbn_competence_two.htm.

National Education Association. (2001). *National Board Certification: A guide for candidates 2000-2001.* Retrieved August 11, 2002, from hppt://www.nea.org/teaching/nbpts/guide.

Neades, B. L. (2003). Professional portfolios: All you need to know and were afraid to ask. *Accident and Emergency Nursing, 11,* 49–55.

Nursing and Midwifery Council (NMC). (2002). *The PREP handbook.* London: NMC.

Oermann, M. (2002). Developing a professional portfolio in nursing. *Orthopaedic Nursing, 21*(2), 73–78.

Pearson, A. (1998). The competent nurse and continuing education: Is there a relationship between the two? *International Journal of Nursing Practice, 4*(3), 143.

Redfern, L., & Hull, C. (1997). Professional development—PREP and profiles: Knowledge for practice. *Nursing Times, 93*(1), 1–4.

Richardson, A. (1998). Personal professional profiles. *Nursing Standard, 12*(38), 35–40.

Royal College of Nursing (RCN). (2003a). *Development planning: Developing your PDP.* Retrieved April 15, 2003, from http://rcn.axia.com/private/learningareas/topic.asp
———. (2003b). *Faculty of Emergency Nursing.* London: RCN.

Ryan, M., & Carlton, K. H. (1997). Portfolio applications in a school of nursing. *Nurse Educator, 22*(1), 35–39.

Salend, S. J. (2001). Creating your own professional portfolio. *Intervention in School and Clinic, 36*(4), 195–201.

Snadden, D., & Thomas, M. (1998). The use of portfolio learning in medical education. *Medical Teacher, 20*(3), 192–199.

Thomas, K., Lamson, S., & King, A. (2001, February 17–21). *Training teacher candidates to create web-based electronic professional portfolios.* Paper presented at the annual meeting of the Association of Teacher Educators, New Orleans, LA.

United Kingdom Central Council for Nurses, Midwives, and Health Visitors (UKCC). (1994). *The future of professional practice: The council's standard for education and practice following registration.* London: UKCC.

Windle, J. (2003). Faculty of emergency nursing. *Emergency Nurse, 10*(10), 5.

Wolf, K. (1996). Developing an effective teaching portfolio. *Educational Leadership, 53*(6), 34–37.

Assembling a Professional Portfolio: An Authentic and Valid Approach to Competency Assessment 4

Karen E. Greco, MN, RN, ANP

Developing Your Portfolio

Developing a professional portfolio is a continuous and reflective process (Day 2001). This self-assessment component of portfolio development helps identify strengths and areas needing growth. Portfolio components will vary depending upon the purpose of the portfolio. Portfolios may be assembled to document one's career accomplishments, to gather evidence that demonstrates knowledge and skill in an area of expertise, or to catalog one's possessions. Professional portfolios are often a collection of documents that validate a person's education and experience in a given field. Portfolios may include the following (Brooks & Madda 1999; Day 2001; Genetic Nursing Credentialing Commission [GNCC] 2003; Meister et al. 2002; Serembus 2000; Williams 2003):

- curriculum vitae
- letters of recommendation
- peer or supervisor evaluations
- proof of licenses and certifications, honors, and awards
- copies of publications, research presentations, continuing education, community activities, and clinical case studies

In nursing, professional portfolios have been used for many different purposes including assessment of student learning (Ball, Daly, & Carnwell 2000; Day 2001; Forker and McDonald 1996), demonstration of professional competence (Ball, Daly, & Carnwell 2000; Whittaker, Carson, & Smolenski 2000), seeking a job or advancing a career (Serembus 2000), academic credit (Day 2001), nursing licensure (Green & Ogden 1999; Serembus 2000), and credentialing in a nursing specialty (Greco & Mahon 2002). A more detailed description of the purposes and uses of portfolios can be found in Chapters 2 and 3.

TABLE 4-1   Components That Could Be Included in a Professional Portfolio

Curriculum Vitae (CV) (listed below are categories often included in a CV)
Contact information
Post–high school education
Professional licenses and certifications
Professional experience
Publications (journal articles, book chapters, books, published abstracts, magazine, newspaper, or newsletter articles, brochures, web page)
Presentations (local, regional, national, international)
Professional activities/memberships
Scholarships
Special achievements, honors, and awards
Research experience and funded grants (if applicable)

Documents Verifying Professional Education
Professional licenses
Professional certifications/credentials
Transcripts
Diplomas
Continuing education certificates

Documents Verifying Publications
Journal article reprint or photocopy
Web link for online publication
Photocopy of newsletter article, book chapter, etc.

Documents Verifying Presentations
Brochure, flyer, or conference agenda
Letter verifying presentation
Picture of a poster session
Published abstract

Documents Verifying Honors, Awards, and Special Achievements
Program listing the award
Letters stating receipt of the award or honor
Photocopy of an award plaque
Photocopy of a news clipping or press release

Documents Verifying Professional Experience and Expertise
Letter from supervisor
Performance evaluation
Letters of recommendation
Case studies

Documents Verifying Community Activities
Letter or other document from the community organization that acknowledges your contribution or service

The portfolio provides evidence of education and professional development (Jasper 1995). Table 4-1 gives an overview of items often included in a professional portfolio. Keep in mind that there is a difference between listing and providing evidence of one's accomplishments. For example, a curriculum vitae itself is merely a list of one's accomplishments. Transcripts, certificates of continuing education contact hours (sometimes referred to as continuing education units [CEUs]), proofs of

TABLE 4-2 Steps in Compiling a Portfolio

Determine the purpose of the portfolio.

Find out the required or recommended portfolio components.

Gather your materials.

Organize your materials so everything is easy to identify and locate.

Present your materials visually pleasing format with a table of contents.

licenses or certifications, and reprints of published articles are examples of evidence of accomplishments. Portfolios used for credentialing, licensure, or as an assessment of student learning will include verifiable evidence of accomplishments.

Compiling Your Portfolio

Determining the Purpose of the Portfolio

The basic steps in compiling a portfolio are outlined in Table 4-2. In preparing a portfolio the first step is to determine the purpose of the portfolio. The purpose will somewhat determine the components. A portfolio to demonstrate student learning will be different from a portfolio used to demonstrate professional competence. Portfolios for assessment of student learning in an educational setting often include a reflective component. The reflective component of portfolio development can bring nursing theory and practice closer together, be a catalyst for learning, and allow students to take control of their own learning needs (McMullan et al. 2003). An example of portfolio components for staff and career development can be found in the work of Brooks and Madda (1999). Serembus (2000) has a good table for professional portfolio evidence. Meister and colleagues (2002) have tables including contents for both student and experienced nurse portfolios. Sample pages from a fictitious GNCC portfolio appear in Appendix C.

Identify Portfolio Contents and Gather Your Materials

The next step is to find out if there is a list of required or recommended portfolio components and a format you need to follow. If so, these guidelines will need to be obtained and followed. You might also ask if there is an example of a successful portfolio that you can use as a model. Make a list of everything you will need. Determine which items will require the most time to accomplish and prioritize them at the top of the list. For example, transcripts need to be ordered from any educational institutions attended, and often there is a fee for this service. This can sometimes be done over the Internet but usually requires a verbal or written request to the educational institution. Letters of recommendation often require lead-time, depending on the schedule of the person you are asking to write a letter. Case logs may need to be verified and signed by a supervisor and, again, you will need to allow time for this person to complete the verification process. Curriculum vitae may need to be updated, but this could be done, for example, while you are waiting for reference letters and transcripts. Once you have your vitae updated, it is a good idea to keep it updated as your career continues to develop.

Organize and Present Your Materials

A professional portfolio contains many important documents that need to be organized, easily updated, and readily accessed. Choose an organizational system that works for you. Options to consider include a three-ring notebook with pocket folders, file folders, or a large accordion file. If there is a list of portfolio requirements, labeling sections to correspond with the list of requirements will facilitate assembly of portfolio components. One option is to use a three-ring notebook view binder, with a plastic sleeve on the front of the notebook where a cover page can be inserted. Include a table of contents so the reader will know what is included and where it can be found. Have a set of dividers with tabs that can be labeled. Pocket folders can be used for brochures, cards, or other documents and small items. Clear page protectors that are three-hole punched can be used for protection copies of certificates, letters, or other one-page documents. When your portfolio is complete, it is a good idea to make a backup copy in case the portfolio is lost or misplaced.

Assembling a Professional Portfolio for Credentialing: The GNCC Example

This section will focus specifically on compiling a professional portfolio using the example of applying to the Genetic Nursing Credentialing Commission (GNCC) for credentialing as an Advanced Practice Nurse in Genetics (APNG) or Genetic Clinical Nurse (GCN). The GNCC portfolio is used in applying for either the APNG or the GCN credential to demonstrate clinical competence as a genetic nurse. What is unique about GNCC credentialing is that it is based on having the applicant submit a professional portfolio rather than performance on one or more exams. A description of how the GNCC portfolio components were determined can be found in Chapter 5, and a description of how the portfolio is evaluated and scored can be found in Chapters 6 and 7. Although GNCC is used as an example, the process can be applied in similar situations where a professional portfolio is needed to document competence.

Obtaining an Application Packet

The first step is to obtain an official APNG or GCN credential application packet. Information on how to obtain an official application packet can be found at the GNCC web site, www.geneticnurse.org. It is advisable to obtain the packet at least three months prior to portfolio submission since the packet contains instructions on how to assemble your portfolio, what you will need to include in your portfolio, forms you will need to use, and selected examples to assist you. GNCC portfolio components are listed in Table 4-3. Purchasing a copy of the *Statement on the Scope and Standards of Genetics Clinical Nursing Practice* (1998) by the International Society of Nurses

T A B L E 4 - 3 Documentation Included in GNCC Portfolio Requirements

Licensure as an RN

A baccalaureate in nursing or equivalent for the GCN or documentation of a master's in nursing or equivalent for the APNG

At least five years' experience as a genetic nurse with 50% genetic practice component for the GCN

Case log form with documentation of 50 cases providing genetic health care in past five years signed by a genetics professional

Four in-depth genetic case histories reflecting ISONG standards of genetics nursing practice at the appropriate level of genetics nursing practice (about four to six pages of text each in addition to a pedigree)

Minimum of 50 contact hours of education in genetics in the past five years for the APNG or 45 hours for the GCN

Three professional letters of reference

Source: Genetic Nursing Credentialing Commission (GNCC) (2003). *Requirements for the APNG and GCN credentials.* Available at http://www.geneticnurse.org.

in Genetics (ISONG) and the American Nurses Association (ANA) is highly recommended when assembling your GNCC portfolio and is available through the ANA web site at www.nursesbooks.org. The evaluation criteria for the GNCC portfolio requirements are based on these standards of genetics nursing practice.

Plan Ahead

Assembling a GNCC professional portfolio is time-consuming. For example, original transcripts will need to be ordered to verify educational degrees and genetic content that was obtained through formal academic coursework. Letters of reference will need to be solicited from supervisors and professional colleagues sufficiently in advance to allow enough time for the letters to be thoughtfully written and returned prior to the portfolio submission deadline. Table 4-4 contains tips for preparing a GNCC portfolio.

Obtaining documentation of having cared for 50 cases (patients and their families) related to genetics nursing practice can be challenging. Ideally, it is best to gather this information prospectively after receiving the application packet containing the necessary forms. It is much easier to evaluate the cases as one cares for the patient rather than gathering this information prospectively (Greco & Mahon 2002). The same is true for writing four in-depth case studies reflecting the ISONG standards of clinical genetics nursing practice. Case studies will need to include the following components: a pedigree showing three (or more) generations of the patient's family and their health patterns, dates of care, narrative patient history, physical assessment

T A B L E 4 - 4 Tips for Preparing Your Portfolio

Obtain a copy of any documents you will need in compiling your portfolio, such as portfolio guidelines or criteria, required portfolio components, and application packets. Retrospectively include brochures from conferences attended and materials from courses taken. Keep copies of handouts from presentations you give, brochures or handouts you create, and articles or other materials you write. Keep a record of honors, awards, and recognitions you receive. If you have questions, find out whom to contact. It is better to ask questions if you are uncertain about requirements than to make assumptions.

of the patient, nursing activities, any relevant correspondence to the patient such as summary letters, patient follow-up, any educational materials prepared for the patient, and outcomes and how they were evaluated. For example, in cancer genetics the case study might include cancer risk factors, cancer surveillance and risk reduction recommendations, psychosocial support, information about genetic testing, and referrals to appropriate genetic and community resources. Maintaining patient confidentiality is essential when compiling case logs and in-depth case studies. All identifying information must be removed from any documents submitted to the GNCC or the portfolio will not be accepted. Removing all personal health information from case logs and case studies is especially important and is a legal requirement under the Privacy Rules of the Health Insurance Portability and Accountability Act (HIPAA) of 1996 (Frank-Stromberg 2003).

Documentation of professional activities is also more easily gathered prospectively. When presenting to a public group or a professional group, it is important to keep copies of the flyer or brochure announcing the talk, outlines, handouts, or other material relating to the program. Newsletter articles, patient education materials, or professional publications related to genetic topics written by the nurse should also be kept. Many nurses are impressed by the volume of materials they have in this component of the portfolio (Greco & Mahon, 2002).

Competency Assessment by Portfolio: Authenticity and Validity

Assessing competency of nursing practice has long been subject to debate (Redman, Lenburg, & Walker 1999; Whittaker, Carson, & Smolenski 2000). How can we ensure that a practicing nurse has met a certain standard of nursing practice? Can a portfolio accurately assess a nurse's competency in a specialty nursing practice? How can we ensure that a portfolio-based assessment is authentic and valid compared to taking an examination? Assessing competency focuses on outcomes with the goal being to evaluate the nurse's performance of effective application of knowledge and skill in the practice setting (Redman, Lenburg, & Walker 1999). Licensure by state boards of nursing entails successful completion of several requirements, including the National Council Licensure Examination (NCLEX), based upon several factors, including up-to-date new graduate job analyses. Credentialing of nurses by professional nursing organizations often utilizes some type of competency-based assessment to ensure that a certain standard of nursing practice has been met.

The Pew Health Professions Commission published two reports challenging state regulatory boards to implement and evaluate continuing competence, which have facilitated nursing's increased focus on this issue (Pew Health Professions Commission 1995, 1998). In 1999, the ANA Board of Directors formed an expert panel to look at this issue and make policy and research recommendations. This expert panel developed a Continuing Professional Nursing Competence Process based on development of a professional portfolio by individual nurses (Whittaker, Carson, & Smolenski 2000). A professional portfolio is one method used to assess competency that is receiving increased attention in nursing.

Current methods for demonstrating initial and continuing competency evaluation include:

- examination
- self-assessment
- peer review
- case review
- supervised clinical practice
- clinical internship
- portfolio
- computer-simulated testing
- reviewed continuing education

Methods for evaluating continuing competency can be found in Chapter 1.

Advantages of Portfolio Based Assessment of Competency

Evaluation by professional portfolio has a number of strengths compared to other methods of competency evaluation. What distinguishes performance-based assessment from objective testing is the ability to measure aspects of a person's behavior, such as performing actual tasks in the work environment or developing a solution to a hypothetical realistic problem (Bradley 1996). Portfolio assessments have the potential for both evaluation and promotion of learning, self-assessment, and documentation of self-growth. In addition, the nurse's ability to think critically and solve problems can be documented (Forker & McDonald 1996). Complex sets of skills that do not lend themselves easily to measurement by exam, such as compiling in-depth case histories, can be evaluated by portfolio. Portfolios in education involve student-centered learning and self-reflection in addition to an opportunity to demonstrate student progress (Ball, Daly, & Carnwell 2000). Good test-taking skills may help when taking an exam but not when compiling a portfolio. Multiple-choice testing places the person in a passive, reactive role and affords a limited capacity to measure higher-order cognitive abilities such as the behavioral aspects of competence and skill required by professional practice (Bradley 1996). A well-constructed portfolio with good evaluation criteria can be a more complete measure of professional competence than an exam.

Addressing Issues of Portfolio Validity

There are no completely objective ways to ensure adequate content validity. Having an expert panel review the portfolio components and exercise judgment concerning their relevancy to what is being measured is one method for verifying content validity (Polit & Hungler 1999). For example, a diverse panel of expert genetic nurses, representing a variety of practice settings and levels of education, reviewed the GNCC portfolio components and based the requirements on the Scope and Standards of Genetics Clinical Nursing Practice (ISONG & ANA 1998). These steps were taken to promote the validity of the portfolio as a method of credentialing.

To be an effective assessment tool, a portfolio must provide information about the quality of a professional's thinking or action, which can be evaluated by professional peers (Bradley 1996). Collecting several diverse pieces of evidence relating to the knowledge and skills required of a competency of outcome can strengthen the validity of the evidence presented (Day 2001). For example, evidence to document the ability to conduct a physical examination could include a validation letter, a write-up of the findings of the exam, and a transcript from a class on physical assessment.

Criterion validity is the assurance that the approach (instrument or method of evaluation) matches a previously established, well-accepted measure or standard of performance. In criterion-referenced testing, the individual's performance is evaluated against criteria provided to the individual so both the individual and the evaluator are clear on what is required (Redman, Lenburg, & Walker 1999). In order for criterion-referenced evaluation to be valid, the criterion needs to be as objective as possible, and there needs to be a relationship between the criterion or criteria being used for the evaluation and the element being measured. This is not always easy with portfolio evaluation. For example, criterion for evaluation of the quality of a professional publication might include whether it was peer reviewed. The criterion or criteria for evaluation of a clinical case study might be published standards of nursing practice. Whenever measurement (imposition of a grade or score, a numerical quantity) is used, the validity of the criterion used strengthens the veracity of the portfolio approach.

The GNCC Professional Portfolio Example

Credentialing of genetic nurses has been available since 2000. The International Society of Nurses in Genetics recognized that genetic nurses needed to have credentialing to establish competency, and a formal credentialing committee, later the Genetic Nursing Credentialing Commission (GNCC) (www.geneticnurse.org), was formed to address this issue. The members of the GNCC include expert genetic nurses and experienced educators. This group convened several standard setting conferences to determine the following:

- credentialing requirements
- components of the GNCC portfolios for the APNG and GCN credentials to reflect those requirements
- genetic competencies based on the ANA and ISONG standards of genetics nursing practice
- portfolio evaluation and scoring criteria

T A B L E 4 - 5 Strengths of the GNCC Portfolio Credentialing Process

Requirements are based on the ISONG/ANA *Statement on the Scope and Standards of Genetics Clinical Nursing Practice.*

Standard-setting conferences of expert nurses were convened to determine credentialing requirements, portfolio components, and evaluation criteria and methodology.

Requirements of other genetic health professionals were considered.

Credentialing requirements, portfolio components, forms to be used, and case history examples are included in the application packet to clarify expectations.

Scoring criteria is clearly identified to the applicant.

Each portfolio is evaluated and scored independently by several members of a specially trained score team.

A special software program for evaluating the portfolios has been developed by scoring professionals.

Much effort has gone into developing a valid credentialing process that is defensible and credible. Since credentialing by exam is the most common method of certification used by specialty nursing organizations, credentialing by portfolio needed to be a rigorous process in order to withstand potential criticism and to be legally defensible. Certification requirements of genetic peers, such as genetic counselors and medical geneticists, were obtained and scrutinized for comparability to the requirements for nursing certification. The GNCC application packets for the APNG and GCN credentials include specific instructions regarding credentialing requirements, portfolio components, forms to be used, and examples so expectations of the applicant and evaluation criteria are clearly identified. Each portfolio is independently evaluated and scored by several members of a specially trained scoring team (Cook et al. 2003). A neural net software scoring program was developed by scoring professionals with input from expert genetic nurses to make the process as objective as possible. The scoring program and process is described in detail in Chapters 5 and 6. The strengths of the GNCC portfolio credentialing process are summarized in Table 4-5.

Verifying Authenticity of Portfolio Components

How does one know that the portfolio components are authentic? Although no system is totally foolproof, there are ways to help ensure that the information submitted is authentic. Nursing licenses can be verified with the appropriate board of nursing. Applicants are asked to send letters of reference or verification from supervisors or professional colleagues in sealed envelopes with a signature across the seal. Applicants are asked to submit selected copies of publications or to provide a web address where a publication can be accessed. Original, sealed transcripts are required. It would be difficult to submit a fraudulent professional portfolio. Even if it were possible, it would be a formidable challenge. For example, how could an applicant create a sealed transcript with the official seal of a university? A common method for authentication of letters is to have the person writing the letter seal the envelope, sign his or her name across the envelope seal, and mail the letter directly to the person or organization requesting the letter. The purpose is to lower the chances of forgery or tampering. Table 4-1 includes several examples of evidence that can help verify the authenticity of portfolio components.

Validation letters can provide an indirect and authenticated account of performance and competence (Day 2001). It is important that these letters identify specific aspects of the outcome or competence being demonstrated. A set of criteria for validation letters can be provided to the person writing the letter to help ensure that the validation letter provides the necessary information. A validation letter needs to include:

- a description of the competence or skill being validated
- a description of how the skill or competence was demonstrated (e.g., test, direct observation)
- a description of the evidence to support the validation (e.g., passed the test, completed the skill according to a guideline or standard)
- a description of the circumstances under which the validation took place (e.g., in a lab or clinic observed by an instructor or part of an inservice at work)
- the name, contact information, and credentials of the person providing the validation letter

An example of a validation letter written by a client can be found in Day 2001. Other examples of validation letters include having a supervisor or professional peer write a letter documenting observation of a clinical skill, or having an instructor write a letter describing an incident demonstrating application of a standard of practice or exercising critical thinking.

Summary

Attention to the choice of both the portfolio components and the portfolio evaluation criteria is critical if the portfolio is to have validity, reliability, and authenticity (credibility and respectability). How effective portfolios are in assessing professional competence is still being debated. Evaluating the efficacy of portfolios is complex because they are used for so many different purposes.

Portfolio evaluation criteria for student learning, professional licensure from a board of nursing, and specialty credentialing by a professional organization are all different. Research looking at how well portfolios relate to outcomes is limited, and validity needs to be reestablished each time portfolio evaluation is used for a different purpose. Taable 4-6 gives an interesting overview of the variety of settings in which evaluation by portfolio is being used. The use of portfolios to evaluate professional competence, especially in the areas of licensure and credentialing, is both innovative and challenging. This is an area where validity and rigor are especially important. The GNCC portfolio evaluation process offers a unique approach to providing rigorous, valid, and authentic assessment of professional portfolios to evalu-

TABLE 4-6 Web Site Resources

For Use of Portfolios in Nursing

Georgia Southern University School of Nursing
http://www2.gasou.edu/nursing/academic_portfolio.html

University of Dundee Distance Learning Nursing and Palliative Care Unit
http://www.dundee.ac.uk/meded/nursing/m14.htm

University of Arkansas School of Nursing
Guidelines for Outcome Portfolio Development
Comprehensive Examination for MNSc Students
http://nursing.uams.edu/portfolioguidelines-02.pdf

National Assembly for Wales HM Prison Service Nursing Portfolio
http://www.doh.gov.uk/prisonhealth/nursingportfolio.pdf

University of Rochester School of Nursing Portfolio Seminar I Course Description
http://www.urmc.rochester.edu/son/academics/nur351

Winona State University Masters in Nursing
Credit by Portfolio: Portfolio Review Process for MS Class Substitution
http://www.winona.edu/nursing/graduate/portfolio.htm

For Credentialing by Portfolio

Genetic Nursing Credentialing Commission
http://www.geneticnurse.org

University of Colorado Hospital Credentialing Procedure
http://www.uch.edu/professionalresources/flash/uexcel/2000-2001%20credentialing%20procedure.htm

Wound Ostomy Continence Nursing Certification Board
Recertification by Professional Growth Plan (portfolio)
http://www.uch.edu/professionalresources/flash/uexcel/2000-2001%20credentialing%20procedure.htm
An organizing binder with a diskette for printing out verification forms is available.

ate professional competence. A similar process could be utilized by other nursing or health professional organizations interested in awarding a professional credential based on portfolio evaluation to determine competence.

References

American Nurses Association (ANA). (2004). *Nursing: Scope and standards of practice.* Washington, DC: ANA.

Ball, E., Daly, W. M., & Carnwell, R. (2000). The use of portfolios in the assessment of learning and competence. *Nursing Standard, 14*(43), 35–37.

Bradley, R. (1996). Fellow of the American Dietetic Association credentialing program: Development and implementation of a portfolio-based assessment. *Journal of the American Dietetic Association, 96*(5), 513–517.

Brooks, B. A., & Madda, M. (1999). How to organize a professional portfolio for staff and career development. *Journal for Nurses in Staff Development [JNSD], 15*(1), 5–10.

Cook, S. S., Kase, R., Middelton, L., & Monsen, R. B. (2003). Portfolio evaluation for professional competence: Credentialing in genetics for nurses. *Journal of Professional Nursing, 19*(2), 85–90.

Day, M. (2001). Developing benchmarks for prior learning assessment. Part 2: Practitioners. *Nursing Standard, 15*(35), 38–44.

Forker, J. E., & McDonald, M. E. (1996). Perspectives on assessment—methodologic trends in the healthcare professions: Portfolio assessment. *Nurse Educator, 21*(5), 9–10.

Frank-Stromborg, M. (2003). They're real and they're here: The new federally regulated privacy rules under HIPAA. *MEDSURG Nursing, 12*(6), 380–385.

Genetic Nursing Credentialing Commission (GNCC). (2003). Requirements for the APNG and GCN credentials. Available online at http://www.geneticnurse.org.

Greco, K. & Mahon, S. (2003). Genetics nursing practice enters a new era with credentialing. *Internet Journal of Advanced Nursing Practice, 5*(2). Available online at http://www.ispub.com/ostia/index.php?xmlfilepath=journals/ijanp/vol5n2/genetics.xml.

Green, A., & Ogden, B. S. (1999, March–April). Three state nursing boards examine continued competency. *The American Nurse, 31*(2), 2.

International Society of Nurses in Genetics (ISONG) & American Nurses Association (ANA). (1998). *Statement on the scope and standards of genetics clinical nursing practice.* Washington, DC: American Nurses Publishing.

Jasper, M. A. (1995). The potential of the professional portfolio for nursing: Maintenance and verification of continuing nursing practice following initial nurse training in the UK. *Journal of Clinical Nursing, 4*(4), 249–255.

McMullan, M., Endacott, R., Gray, M., Jasper, M., Miller, C., Scholes, J. & Webb, C. (2003). Portfolios and assessment of competence: a review of the literature. *Journal of Advanced Nursing, 41*(3), 283–294.

Meister, L., Heath, J., Andrews, J., & Tingen, M. S. (2002). Professional nursing portfolios: A global perspective. *MEDSURG Nursing, 11*(4), 177–182.

Pew Health Professions Commission (1995). *Performing health care workforce regulation: Policy considerations for the 21st century.* San Francisco: University of California San Francisco Center for the Health Professions.

———. (1998). *Strengthening consumer protection: Priorities for health care workforce regulation.* San Francisco: University of California San Francisco Center for the Health Professions.

Polit, D. F., & Hungler, B. P. (1999). *Nursing research: Principles and methods.* 6th ed. Philadelphia: Lippincott.

Redman, R. W., Lenburg, C. B., & Walker, P. H. (1999). Competency assessment: Methods for development and implementation in nursing education. *Online Journal of Issues in Nursing.* Available online at http://www.nursingworld.org/ojin/topic10/tpc10_4.htm.

Serembus, J. F. (2000). Teaching the process of developing a professional portfolio. *Nurse Educator, 25*(6), 282–287.

Trossman, S. (1999). The professional portfolio: Documenting who you are, what you do. *American Nurse, 31*(2), 1–3.

Whittaker, S., Carson, W., & Smolenski, M. C. (2000, June 30). Assuring continued competence—policy questions and approaches: How should the profession respond? *Online Journal of Issues in Nursing.* Available online at http://www.nursingworld.org/ojin/topic10/tpc10_4.htm.

Williams, M. (2003). Assessment of portfolios in professional education. *Nursing Standard, 18*(8), 33–37.

Developing a Credential Based Upon Portfolio Evidence 5

Rita Black Monsen, DSN, MPH, RN, FAAN; Sarah Sheets Cook, MEd, RNC;
Lindsay Middelton, BSN, RN, CGC; and Ron Kase, MBA, BSN, RN

Background: Nursing Education in Genetics

Genetic technology transfer to health care has proliferated in the past decade such that genetic testing for certain forms of heart disease, cancer, muscular dystrophies, and other conditions affecting significant population segments is nearly commonplace today. The identification of carriers for cystic fibrosis has entered services to pregnant women as a community standard of care (American College of Obstetrics and Gynecology 2001). Indeed, a new role for nurses in the era of health care based upon genomics appears on the horizon, one in which nurses assess families for risk of inherited illness, provide information about appropriate genetic screening and testing, provide counseling, and coordinate care with a variety of providers in communities (Lea & Monsen 2003).

Attention to genetics in undergraduate, graduate, and continuing education in nursing has undergone considerable growth in the past five years. A number of efforts by leaders in nursing education have resulted in the addition of courses in basic genetics and molecular biology in baccalaureate programs (Zamerowski 2000), and clinical genetics in nursing coursework (Horner et al. 2004; Prows et al. 1999). A small number of graduate programs preparing advanced practice nurses (clinical nurse specialists and nurse practitioners) for roles in genetic services have been operating for over ten years, but an increasing number of schools of nursing have begun adding clinical genetics to existing master's and doctoral programs in the past five years. Perhaps most significant is the appearance of multiple continuing education initiatives to expand the genetic knowledge base of nurse clinicians, educators, and researchers (Lea, Feetham, & Monsen 2002). Some of these efforts have sprung from national centers (the National Cancer Institute, the National Human Genome Research Institute, the National Institute for Nursing Research), and others have come from regional academic and clinical centers (the University of Illinois, the University of Iowa, Columbia University, the University of Cincinnati, the City of Hope, the Fox Chase Cancer Center, and the Foundation for Blood Research). Nurses have received these offerings enthusiastically; and together with the proliferation of gene-based technologies in health care, the expanded access to education in genetics has created new career opportunities for qualified clinicians.

Launching the Credential for Advanced Practice Nurses and Generalist-Level Nurses

The initial groundwork for establishing the credential in genetics for advanced practice nurses was laid with the 1998 publication *Scope and Standards of Genetics Clinical Nursing Practice*, developed by representatives from the International Society of Nurses in Genetics, Inc. (ISONG), the American Nurses Association (ANA), and the American Nurses Credentialing Center (ANCC). The ISONG/ANA *Scope and Standards* document was based on the ANA *Scope and Standards of Clinical Nursing Practice* (ANA 1998) and delineated the roles and practice boundaries of nurse generalists (baccalaureate-prepared, able to practice in a wide variety of healthcare arenas) and advanced practice nurses (master's or doctorally prepared nurses, able to practice at an expert level in healthcare settings with a focus on genetics). The ANA published its revised *Scope and Standards of Nursing Practice* in 2004, and the ISONG/ANA *Statement on the Scope and Standards of Genetics Clinical Nursing Practice* is currently being updated to reflect both changes in genetics nursing practice and the content and format of the revised ANA standards (ANA 2004; ISONG/ANA 2005).

The ISONG board of directors formed a credentialing committee in 1999 (later the Genetic Nursing Credentialing Commission, Inc. or GNCC) and provided funding for the development of procedures leading to the Advanced Practice Nurse in Genetics (APNG) credential, first awarded in 2001. In 2002, a second credential, the Genetics Clinical Nurse (GCN) credential, was offered in response to ISONG member requests using the APNG pattern. Nurses with a baccalaureate degree and experience in healthcare settings with a genetics component were becoming more numerous and enthusiastic about a credential in genetics nursing. The design of the GCN (the baccalaureate-level credential) was patterned after that of the APNG, and used the ISONG and ANA *Standards* document to guide design of the performance indicators appropriate for the generalist nurse practicing in genetics who does not have the responsibilities for independent decision-making, genetic counseling, education of other professionals, and conduct of research. The policies for the GCN are based upon a portfolio of evidence paralleling those of the APNG, with the two credentials being awarded since 2002. Appendix B contains sample pages from the GNCC Application Guidelines Packet, including the requirements for the APNG credential. The GNCC web site, www.geneticnurse.org, provides information about the credentials, lists nurses with the APNG and the GCN, and offers assistance with application and mentors for portfolio assembly.

Design of the Requirements for the APNG and GCN Credentials

During its first two years of operation, the GNCC members deliberated on the requirements for an advanced practice nursing credential for clinicians in specialty genetic healthcare settings. The GNCC leadership conducted an intense search of the literature, an examination of advanced practice nursing characteristics and educational requirements from the American Nurses Association and other clinical specialty organizations, and a review of the regulations for advanced practice nursing from the National Council of State Boards of Nursing. These documents and related resources contributed to the nexus of the educational and experiential requirements for the first credential. In addition, consultation with professional organizations in genetics (the National Society of Genetic Counselors and the American Boards of Medical Genetics and Genetic Counseling) and consumer support (the Genetic Alliance) added features to the required components so that the credentialed nurse in genetics could expect to receive recognition commensurate with that of colleagues in this specialty field. Because the GNCC leadership included nurses with American Board of Medical Genetics certification, steps were taken to ensure respectability of the GNCC credential among other health professionals with certification in genetics. Finally, because the GNCC leadership had nurses with regulatory board experience, clear verification procedures (including random selection of components for substantiation of evidence, verification of origin of documents, and validation of currency of licenses and certifications) were included in the design of the portfolio and the process of receiving, evaluating, and managing the credentialing work.

The GNCC leadership knew that the financial resources and the available pool of potential candidates for development of a valid and reliable examination were inadequate (projected cost of developing a 100-item examination was $40,000, estimated by M. Smolenski in June 1999). They recognized that ISONG could not pay for costly exam development and beta-testing and that a more informal approach to exam development would be subject to security challenges and lack of psychometric integrity. They therefore pursued the option of designing the requirements and listing a verifiable compendium of documents that would compose a portfolio leading to the award of a credential in genetics nursing. The expenditures by ISONG for establishment of the APNG credential totaled $19,000 (first years of operation until award of initial credentials in September 2001). As of August 2004 the total expenditures for all of the years of operation (including recruitment and training of GNCC Score Team members, management of portfolio submissions and awards, and coordination of GNCC operations) was $43,000. Future projections for expanded web site operations for online management of the portfolio submissions, technical consultation, and marketing to wider audiences of nurses who are increasingly becoming involved in genetic questions in health care will entail fundraising, careful planning, and management of GNCC resources.

The portfolio approach was expected to be authentic because of its demonstration of the applicant's career in nursing (especially the patterns of practice evident in the clinical log and the four in-depth case studies taken from the clinical log). This approach has the advantage of validity by virtue of the genetics nursing competencies developed from the ISONG/ANA *Statement on the Scope and Standards of Genetics Clinical Nursing Practice.* And last, the portfolio requirements have validity based upon their design by expert genetics nurse clinicians and educators (the members of the GNCC who designed the original requirements and continue to monitor them as experience with portfolio evidence grows). The GNCC leadership built in reliability of portfolio evaluation and scoring by virtue of the ongoing annual training cycles of the GNCC Score Teams (see Chapter 3). One component of the training is the annual retreat conducted solely for discussion of the portfolio submissions, the ratings of the components awarded by the Score Team members, and final decision-making about overall pass or fail scores. A *Portfolio Evaluation and Scoring Guide* (GNCC 2002) is used and updated throughout the training process. Interim discussions of portfolio policies and procedures are conducted online with Score Team members. Moreover, the technical support (see the discussion on neural net technology below and in Chapter 7) provides the GNCC the assurance that the range of individual portfolio component scores and patterns of scoring are analyzed and balanced to minimize the influence of any extreme score values.

After these assurances and protections had been incorporated into the portfolio process, the GNCC contracted with a firm specializing in evaluation of professionals based upon performance competencies, the Center for Sustained Leadership, LLC (CSL). The CSL president was found by one of the GNCC leaders in discussions of professional activities at a work-related meeting. This organization, dedicated to training programs that promote self-evaluation of job performance, was supportive of the selection of a portfolio of evidence as the method for evaluating the performance and practice skills of the candidates for the APNG rather than using traditional examination-based approaches. CSL provided consultation on development of the Performance Indicators (measurable competencies) and the technological support for the portfolio evaluation and scoring using neural net software, a computer-based form of determining an outcome based upon multiple layers of data. The neural net software used by the CSL evolved from neural networks, a form of computer-based artificial intelligence that imitates human thinking and brain activity (Hanson & Marshall 2001). In the case of the GNCC credentialing process using portfolios, the neural net technology derives a pass or fail score based upon the values of the various portfolio components assigned by scorers as well as the patterns of scorer judgments on all of the portfolios over time. To date (as of the 2003 credentialing cycle), the GNCC has seen a 98% accuracy rate in scoring pattern analysis by neural net software, meaning that while there is a range of scores entered by the individual scorers evaluating multiple portfolio components, the vast majority of scores follow a solidly congruent pattern. In conclusion, the GNCC has achieved a sound, cost-effective credentialing process based upon portfolios that serves its mission of recognizing genetics nurses' knowledge, practice patterns, and attitudes, benefiting both the parent organization, ISONG, and the pool of candidates from across the spectrum of health care today.

Developing Performance Indicators for Evaluation of Portfolio Evidence

A task force of the credentialing committee consulted with the CSL to derive the essential performance indicators from the ISONG/ANA *Scope and Standards* document. These required characteristics of the performance indicators included measurability, detectability in case study texts, and veracity (integrality with the original standard). All of the ISONG/ANA Standards of Practice were assigned performance indicators, and these were used to derive the areas to be scored in each portfolio submitted. An excerpt of the Performance Indicator as derived from the ISONG/ANA standards document (ISONG & ANA 1998, p. 9) appears on page 63.

The following excerpt from a case study (all names and identifying information have been changed to protect the confidentiality of this family) submitted in a portfolio application for the APNG illustrates several of the features required (more comprehensive case studies are included elsewhere in this book):

Case Study (A.R.)
Date of Visit: March
Risk Identification—Genetic

History of Present Condition
A.R. is an 11-and-8/12ths-year-old white male with a previous diagnosis of neurofibromatosis, type 1 (NF-1). Since we last saw him in May of the previous year, his parents told us that he has been in good health. He has had no significant illnesses and no hospitalizations. He is not taking any medications at present.

His parents describe that his teachers noted a "new bump" on his left forehead, and that they were concerned that this might be a neurofibroma. Furthermore, they told us that A.R. has been complaining of headaches off and on, as many as two per week. They had additional questions about what to expect with puberty in terms of symptoms of NF-1.

Past Medical History
Neurology: At our visit in May, we noted that A.R. had a nodule on his left foot that was causing him discomfort when wearing shoes. We referred him and the family to the Neurofibromatosis Clinic, Boston, for further evaluation, an overall plan, and follow-up. Unfortunately, A.R. was ill on the day of his consultation, and the family did not have the opportunity to have the nodule evaluated by Dr. K., orthopedic specialist, on the day of the visit. Since the last visit, the parents report

that the nodule has remained about the same size and is no longer causing A.R. any discomfort.

Ophthalmology: A.R. is followed by Dr. L., ophthalmologist. We received a copy of Dr. L.'s report of November. He did not note any evidence in A.R. of Lisch nodules, or optic nerve pallor or elevation to suggest a retrobulbar process. A.R. does wear glasses for a refractive error. His glasses were changed by Dr. L. during that visit to accommodate his vision. A.R. is due for a follow-up visit in the fall.

Cardiovascular: At our last visit we noted that A.R.'s blood pressure was elevated at 120/90. We referred him to Dr. M., a pediatric nephrologist, for further evaluation. At his visit with Dr. M. in June, his blood pressure was normal. Dr. M. recommended a renal ultrasound, which the parents say was done and was normal.

A.R. is not taking any prescribed medications at present. Immunizations are up-to-date.

Review of Systems
A.R. has no history of visual loss, deafness, or hearing loss. There is no history of a heart murmur or other cardiac symptoms or abnormalities. There are no symptoms suggestive of hyper- or hypothyroidism or growth hormone deficiency. A.R. does not have a history of shortness of breath, asthma, or other respiratory problems. There is no history of GI/GU symptoms. Specifically, he does not have a history of recurrent constipation, diarrhea, or urinary tract infections. A.R. does not have a history of fractures, joint hypermobility, or other orthopedic problems. There is no history of muscle pain or weakness. There is no history of anemia or unusual bleeding.

Developmental History
A.R. is currently in the fifth grade. He has a special reading teacher and spends time in the Resource Room. He is receiving occupational therapy two times per week and speech therapy three times per week. His parents told us that they feel his speech has improved. A.R. is a member of a youth group, the school band, and a church choir.

Family History
A three-generation family history was reviewed and updated. The following issues of significance were noted:

- Mrs. R. was diagnosed to have uterine cancer in December. She is undergoing radiation therapy in preparation for surgery. Her family history is significant for breast cancer in her late mother, who died at age 38 years, and "stomach cancer" in one of her mother's siblings whose health status is unknown. She has an older sister whose health status is unknown to Mrs. R. This is a significant cancer family history. Mrs. R.'s father, age 68, has hypertension.

A.R.'s maternal grandparents are of Eastern European ancestry. His paternal grandparents' ancestry is not known. There is no known history of consanguinity.

Objective Data

A.R. was cheerful and interactive. He continues to have speech delays, but these have improved since we saw him previously. His mother and father expressed their concerns about A.R.'s new "bump on the head." They told us that they were anxious to know what to do next.

Physical examination:

Height: 52.5 inches (3rd percentile)

Weight: 72.5 pounds (25th percentile)

Head Circumference: 55.5 cm (98th percentile)

Blood Pressure: Left arm 110/80 sitting

General Appearance: A.R. is a well-developed, well-nourished 11-and-8/12th-year-old white male with numerous café-au-lait spots. He was polite and cooperative throughout the examination.

Skin: As previously noted, there is freckling on the neck, and bilateral axillary freckling. There are multiple large and small café-au-lait spots on the chest, back, buttocks, legs, and feet. There is a small neurofibroma palpated on the left upper forehead; and, as previously reported, a soft 1.3-cm nodule on the inner aspect of the left foot. The size of this nodule has not changed since A.R.'s previous visit in May.

Hair: Normal in texture and distribution

HEENT:

Head:	Relatively macrocephalic with a prominent forehead
Eyes:	Slightly down-slanting palpebral fissures and widely set eyes
	Inner canthal distance: 3.5 cm (97th percentile)
	Outer canthal distance: 8.8 cm (75th percentile)
Ears:	Normal placement and position, normal architecture
Nose:	Normal in shape and size
Mouth:	Normal palate; uvula widened and square in shape
Chin:	Unremarkable
Neck:	Relatively short; no masses, webbing, or lesions
Chest:	Symmetric; lungs clear to auscultation bilaterally
Heart:	Regular rhythm and rate; S_1, S_2 normal; pulses full and equal
Abdomen:	No hepatosplenomegaly or masses
Genitalia:	Normal male genitalia; bilaterally descended testes; no pubic or axillary hair
Back:	Right shoulder appears slightly higher than the left but there is no obvious scoliotic curve of the spine

R FAMILY PEDIGREE

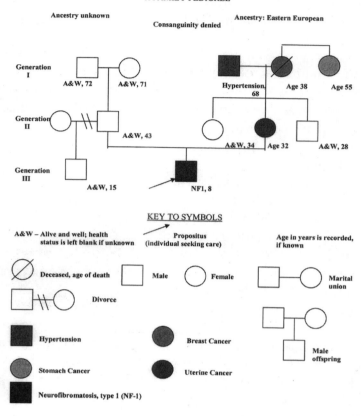

Ancestry unknown

Consanguinity denied

Ancestry: Eastern European

Generation I

A&W, 72   A&W, 71   Hypertension, 68   Age 38   Age 55

Generation II

A&W, 43   A&W, 34   Age 32   A&W, 28

Generation III

A&W, 15   NF1, 8

KEY TO SYMBOLS

A&W – Alive and well; health status is left blank if unknown

Propositus (individual seeking care)

Age in years is recorded, if known

Deceased, age of death   Male   Female   Marital union

Divorce

Hypertension   Breast Cancer   Male offspring

Stomach Cancer   Uterine Cancer

Neurofibromatosis, type 1 (NF-1)

Extremities: Full range of motion, symmetric; bridged crease on the right palm
Nails unremarkable, neurofibroma on the left foot as noted above

Neurologic: Alert, interactive
Cranial nerves: Pupils equally reactive to light, full extra ocular movements
Symmetric facies
Deep tendon reflexes equal and symmetric
Normal muscle tone and strength

Social History

A.R. lives with his parents. He has a maternal uncle who is 28 years old who lives out of state. He has a half brother who lives with his biological mother (Mr. R.'s former wife) in the South.

Family Profile

A.R. and his family live in a small town about two and a half hours north of our clinic. Their home is in a trailer park. A.R.'s father is a music teacher at the local high school. A.R.'s mother is at home. Mrs. R. told us at this visit that she was recently diagnosed to have uterine cancer. She was in the middle of radiation treatment prior to surgery. She told us that she does not have any family around. She and her only sister are estranged and her mother is no longer living. Mr. R.'s parents are alive and well.

Case study continues to describe the nursing care, counseling, referral to community agencies and family support resources as well as follow-up over the following two years.

STANDARD I	
Assessment	
The client and the family affected by or at risk for a genetic condition are assessed by the genetics nurse to identify risk factors and intervention, information, service, and referral needs.	
PERFORMANCE INDICATOR	**CHARACTERISTIC COMPONENTS EXPECTED IN CASE STUDY TEXTS**
I-1 Collect comprehensive client information	1. Biophysical status using dysmorphology examination (assessment of abnormal physical features, if present)/genetic testing results and routine laboratory tests. 2. Coping and adaptation patterns by patient and/or family. 3. Cultural, community, and family support systems. 4. Economic, environmental, and health policy factors affecting health status. 5. History in standard pedigree format for at least three generations. 6. Medical history inclusive but not limited to prenatal, perinatal, and neonatal histories as appropriate. 7. Family integrity, structure, and level of functioning. 8. Growth and development status. 9. Health beliefs and practices of patient and/or family. 10. Psychological, spiritual, values, and beliefs status. 11. Strengths of individual patient and/or family. 12. Risk factors associated with genetic conditions or birth defects. 13. Include health-related goals, roles, and responsibilities in discussion. 14. Discuss data assessment and analysis with client and family 15. Identify patient's and/or family's expectations and needs for care and education 16. Considers ethical, legal, and social issues. 17. Documents information in standard format (for example, the use of assessment terms and narrative format commonly accepted in healthcare settings).

Documenting Professional Role Performance

The GNCC members recognized the importance of clinical competency and used the ISONG and ANA *Standards* documents to derive Performance Indicators for evaluating nursing care with patients and families. They also recognized the importance of genetics nurses being able to apply the Standards of Professional Performance Indicators, based on the ANA *Scope and Standards of Nursing Practice* (ANA 1998, 2004), to genetics nursing practice (ISONG & ANA 1998), which described the role of the nurse as a professional in an interdisciplinary team.

Measurement of these practice standards created some challenges. The GNCC members recognized that a performance appraisal from the place of employment was not likely to elicit ratings comparable to the ISONG standards and would likely be an invasion of the privacy of the applicants. Therefore, these ISONG professional performance standards (including collegiality, ethics, resource utilization, and research) were incorporated into a rating scale document that would be given to employers, administrators, and professional colleagues. At least one of the raters is required to be a genetics health professional, i.e. an MD or PhD geneticist, a Certified Genetic Counselor (American Board of Genetic Counseling credential, abbreviated as CGC), an APNG, or a doctorally prepared nurse with training in genetics. These colleagues were directed to rate the nurse applicant and place the form in a sealed envelope (with their signature on the flap) to be included in the portfolio of evidence. These ratings were to be signed and contact information was to be provided so that the GNCC Score Team could independently verify the ratings as part of the portfolio evaluation process. See an example of this form in Appendix C.

Initial Evaluative Efforts by the GNCC

Three surveys have been conducted by the GNCC to monitor the value of the credential to the genetics nurses and to their employers. The findings of the survey of credentialed nurses revealed that the assembly of their portfolios is challenging (gathering the required documents, constructing the clinical logs and case studies), time-consuming, and costly. Respondents commented on how satisfying the final portfolio was in terms of their sense of professional accomplishment and pride. The first group of credentialed nurses (N = 8 respondents from an initial contact of 13 nurses; all of the currently credentialed nurses practice in genetics healthcare settings) reported that while the Application Guidelines Packet was helpful in preparing their portfolios, they needed several weeks or months to assemble the required materials. A range of estimates of cost in portfolio assembly was $150 to $385, as reported by the respondents. The costs of portfolio assembly included sending for transcripts, duplication of necessary materials, notary signature validation, and postage for submission of the portfolio. Some respondents included the $50 fee for the guidelines themselves in their costs. Despite these comments, the respondents expressed their appreciation for the development of the credential, the opportunity to reflect on their careers, and the expectation that this credential would be valued in the workplace.

A second survey of the employers of credentialed nurses was conducted in June 2003. Of the 20 nurses requested to pass the survey questionnaire to their administrators, approximately 10 responses were received. Two administrators were marginally supportive of the fact that the nurse had achieved the credential. While it was difficult to speculate on the meaning of their sparse comments, the GNCC leadership concluded that perhaps these administrators were not aware of the contribution of the nurses in their settings. A number of other administrators offered strongly positive responses. One remarked that if a value was to be placed on the credential in the system, it might be comparable to the annual salary of the nurse ($80,000). Several administrators were very proud of the nurse and the GNCC credential because it added to the credibility of their clinical program and enhanced the qualifications of their staff when applying for grant and foundation funding.

A third survey was completed in the spring of 2004 to gauge the value of the GNCC credentials to the members of ISONG and nurses in the Oncology Nursing Society, Cancer Genetics Special Interest Group (ONS). A total of 119 responses were received (83 from ISONG members, a 28% response rate, and 26 from ONS, an 18% response rate). Nearly all of the respondents (96%) affirmed the value of the credentials, and a majority reported their intention to apply for one of the credentials in the future. The availability of a mentor was valuable to most of the respondents. The barriers to seeking the credentials most often cited by the respondents included the cost of application ($50 for guidelines packet, $400 application fee for ISONG members, $550 for non–ISONG members), the requirements (degrees in nursing, experience in genetics nursing), and the timing of the submission deadline (annually on March 1). A significant number of respondents were certified in other areas (39% of ISONG members and 77% of ONS members). These results suggest that the GNCC credentials, like many certifications in nursing, are valued by nurses and pose a challenge to those who seek to publicly affirm their expertise for the patients and families they serve as well as their colleagues in healthcare delivery. The GNCC also plans to survey patients and families, consumers of nursing care by nurses credentialed by our organization.

An additional confirmation of the value of the GNCC credentialing program, albeit indirect evidence, is the listing of nurses with the APNG on the web site www.genetests.org, an information clearinghouse about gene-based illnesses and related conditions and clinical resource directory funded by the National Institutes of Health. The administrators of the web site recognized the importance of having nurse clinicians knowledgeable about genetics in the national arena of healthcare delivery and, after examination of the requirements for the APNG credential and discussion with leaders in genetics health care, added these credentialed nurses to their Clinical Directory listing. Nurses with the APNG are the only group of nursing professionals so included in this web site, along with board-certified physician geneticists, genetics counselors, and laboratory-based scientists.

Conclusions

The GNCC has found that the process of awarding the APNG and the GCN credentials based upon a portfolio of verifiable evidence is psychometrically sound and affordable for the parent organization (ISONG). The bases for the portfolio requirements and training of the Score Teams were firmly rooted upon intense discussions and familiarity with the ISONG and ANA *Statement on the Scope and Standards of Genetics Clinical Nursing Practice.* The portfolio approach to credentialing has been a success for our organization in that it does demonstrate the clinical competence of the applicant based upon the documentation submitted, and in that it lends itself to the flexibility necessary when offering certification to nurses whose practices reflect a variety of specialized knowledge and clinical skills.

The first 3 cohorts, totaling 19 candidates for the APNG and 4 candidates for the GCN, submitted portfolios with satisfactory evidence in 2001, 2002, and 2003 (in some instances very superior content, indicating exceptional performance in professional practice). It is likely that a small number of future applicants may not have these strong qualifications, but the GNCC policies recognize that if initial submissions are not successful, nurses interested in the APNG or the GCN credential can be given guidance for reapplication. A most gratifying sign of success has been the fact that all of the nurses who achieved the APNG and the GCN have volunteered to assist with further development of the credentialing process and/or mentoring of future candidates. Indeed, a group of 3 credentialed nurses with the have formed the GNCC Support Team in 2003 and have been prepared to offer informational assistance to future applicants for GNCC credentials. And finally, a number of individuals and organizations have expressed interest in the ISONG experience with the portfolio process and in the APNG and the GCN. The ANA and ANCC have expressed an interest in planning further collaboration with the GNCC toward development of the portfolio process for certification of nurses in other clinical specialties.

Recommendations

Based on the material presented in this chapter, we recommend the following in the development of a credential-based portfolio:

1. Evaluation of the process of awarding the APNG and the GCN based upon a portfolio of verifiable evidence should be continually monitored over time with the neural net software and additional indicators such as career impact, employer satisfaction, patient and family satisfaction, and outcomes of patient care. The cost-effectiveness of the APNG and GCN credentials should be measured both for the parent organization (ISONG and the GNCC) and for the nurses who are potential applicants. Continuing to validate the GNCC

portfolio credentialing process is key to maintaining the integrity of this form of certification in nursing.

2. Comparison of the portfolio outcomes with examination-based outcomes among nurses is necessary to establish criterion validity of the APNG and GCN portfolio process.

3. While the preparation of the Score Teams (2001–2003) for evaluation of the portfolios was based on experiences in development of the procedures and competencies, training of future Score Teams must be evaluated and updated on a consistent basis.

4. The development of the portfolio process for online management is essential for ease of submission, evaluation, and record management. Indeed, the current procedures of online score submission are the first step toward administration of the GNCC credential already in place. The GNCC projects that submission of nearly all the documents, possibly including proof of licensure and certification, transcripts, teaching and educational materials, and evidence of research utilization and publication, can be accomplished online at the present time. Indeed, security protections for ratings by employers, peers, and professional colleagues can be built into the submission process, as can posting of the curriculum vitae, the clinical log, and the four case studies by the applicant. These steps are planned for the future.

5. The explosion of genomics, the coordinated interplay of all of the genes in an individual's DNA makeup that results in various states of health and illness (Pharmaceutical Research and Manufacturers of America 2000), is expected to proliferate in health care in the next five to ten years with everything from gene-based diagnostics to genetically engineered pharmaceuticals and treatments. The nursing profession will recognize the need for counseling and support to large populations of patients and families with new concerns about how their genetic makeup affects their health and risk for illness. Moreover, there is a growing demand under way for all healthcare providers to incorporate genetics into their knowledge bases. And finally, marketing of a GNCC credential for master's- and baccalaureate-prepared nurses who practice in a wide variety of healthcare settings will be central for nursing to maintain its key position in an industry that stands to expand exponentially in the future.

References

American College of Obstetrics and Gynecology. (2001). *Preconception and prenatal carrier screening for cystic fibrosis.* Washington, DC: Author.

American Nurses Association. (1998). *Scope and standards of clinical nursing practice.* 2nd ed. Washington, DC: American Nurses Publishing.

———. (2004). *Scope and standards of nursing practice.* Washington, DC: American Nurses Publishing.

Genetic Nursing Credentialing Commission (GNCC). 2002. *Portfolio evaluation and scoring guide*. GNCC.

Hanson, C. W., & Marshall, B. E. (2001). Artificial intelligence applications in the intensive care unit. *Critical Care Medicine, 29*, 427–435.

Horner, S. D., Abel, E., Taylor, K., & Sands, D. (2004). Using theory to guide the diffusion of genetics content in nursing curricula. *Nursing Outlook, 52*, 80–84.

International Society of Nurses in Genetics, Inc., (ISONG) & American Nurses Association (ANA). (1998). *Statement on the scope and standards of genetics clinical nursing practice*. Washington, DC: American Nurses Publishing.

Lea, D. H., Feetham, S. L., & Monsen, R. B. (2002). Genomic-based healthcare in nursing: A bi-directional approach to bringing genetics into nursing's body of knowledge. *Journal of Professional Nursing, 18*, 120–129.

Lea, D. H., & Monsen, R. B. (2003). Preparing nurses for a new role in 21st century genomics-based health care. *Nursing Education Perspectives, 24*, 75–80.

Pharmaceutical Research and Manufacturers of America. (2000). The genomic lexicon. Available online at http://genomics.phrma.org/lexicon/g.html.

Prows, C. A., Latta, K., Hetteberg, C., Williams, J. K., Kenner, C., & Monsen, R. B. (1999). Preparation of undergraduate nursing faculty to incorporate genetics content into curricula. *Biological Research for Nursing, 1*, 108–112.

Zamerowski, S. T. (2000). A model for integrating genetics into nursing education. *Nursing & Health Care Perspectives, 21*, 298–304.

Preparing Score Teams for Evaluation of Portfolios 6

Nancy R. Bowers, MSN, RN, CNS
Joanna Spahis, MSN, RN, APNG

The management of the portfolio evaluation entails training the reviewers who receive the portfolio submissions, judge the evidence indicating the qualifications of the applicants, and decide whether to award the credential or certification of competence. In the case of the Genetic Nursing Credentialing Commission (GNCC), a Score Team comprises reviewers who are responsible for receiving the portfolios, assigning scores to their contents in areas where a relative value can be placed on the quality of the evidence, and coming to an agreement about the credential award. Some of the documents in the GNCC portfolios, such as the nursing license, do not lend themselves to assigning a score but affirm the applicant's permission from a regulatory body to practice nursing. Other documents such as peer reviews, clinical logs, and case studies can be scrutinized for quality and adherence to the standards of practice of the International Society of Nurses in Genetics (ISONG) and the American Nurses Association (ANA) (1998) and thus assigned a relative value (see discussion below about assignment of scores and Chapters 7 and 8 on evaluation of portfolios and neural net technology). In this chapter, two GNCC Score Team members describe the training and guidelines used for evaluating the portfolios submitted by nurses seeking the Advanced Practice Nurse in Genetics (APNG) or the Genetics Clinical Nurse (GCN) credentials.

Qualifications of the Score Team

A variety of backgrounds in genetics and education are required in the composition of the GNCC Score Teams. Portfolios can be received from applicants with a variety of genetic clinical backgrounds and with varying educational preparation. Each Score Team member is expected to have experience in one or more areas of genetics nursing. This may include, for example, pediatrics, cancer, or prenatal genetics. In addition, a variety of nursing roles are also represented on the Score Teams, including several clinicians, educators, and researchers. This gives the Score Team as a whole the ability to fairly assess the material presented in each portfolio. For example, those Score Team members most familiar with the clinical management of cases in a particular specialty area are most capable of verifying the facts and currency of the counseling strategies used in the case studies presented in the portfolios.

The variety of nursing roles and backgrounds represented on the Score Team can have an effect on the importance that scorers place on various facets of the portfolio. For example, a clinician may focus on accuracy of the facts presented, while an educator might place more emphasis on how strongly the applicant's practice examples follow the nursing process and the ISONG standards, the approach used in the case studies, or the overall style and format of presentation. The clinician might give greater weight to the depth of counseling, the variety of diagnoses seen by the applicant, or the extent that the applicant works as part of an interdisciplinary team. The educator might be more interested in seeing evidence of educational courses taken or lectures given by the applicant, or a greater involvement in research and publication. In our experience, by including a wide variety of genetics nursing specialties and nursing roles on the Score Team, these tendencies toward one preference or another will be balanced in the final outcome decision about the award of the credentials.

The commitment to the Score Team is to serve a three-year term with a third of the scorers rotating in and out every year. This provides the opportunity for the more experienced scorers to teach and share their insight with newer Score Team members, and it gives the newer members confidence in their new role. Newly credentialed genetics nurses are approached by the GNCC leaders and invited to serve as future Score Team members. Newly credentialed nurses often become Score Team members and can provide valuable insight to the nuances of assembling a portfolio from the applicant's point of view. Since the term of service on the Score Team is three years and the credential is valid for five years, newly credentialed nurses are able to serve on the Score Team before having to consider renewal of their credential.

Score Team Training

Score Team training is a combination of on-site and independent, self-directed learning. Because Score Team members must render a judgment about an applicant's practice from the contents of the applicant's portfolio, the Score Team's work is based on a high degree of familiarity with and knowledge about the criteria set for scoring. Score Teams receive on-site training in the scoring process using the *Portfolio Evaluation and Scoring Training Manual* (GNCC 2003), which contains the Performance Indicators, the GNCC Application Guidelines Packet (to provide the basis upon which the applicant created the portfolio), and samples of previous portfolio submissions with commentary as to score assignments. This on-site training session is held early in the year prior to the submission deadline for the receipt of portfolios from applicants (March 1, annually). Training is provided to the incoming Score Team members by the incumbent members.

The scoring process is categorized into several areas. The scorers use specific core indicators during the evaluation of the clinical practice features of the applicant's portfolio. These core indicators are based on ISONG and the ANA's *Statement on the Scope and Standards of Genetics Clinical Nursing Practice* (1998). The major categories for examination of the portfolio include the applicant's (1) clinical practice background, (2) formal and informal education, (3) teaching and educational efforts, and (4) other professional achievements. The documents within the portfolio submitted by the applicant are subject to random verification (for example, checking the curriculum vitae) by the GNCC Score Team members. The ISONG/ANA standards are being revised, and the GNCC core indicators will undergo review after publication of the revised ISONG/ANA standards to ensure consistency with the new document.

The case studies in the portfolio form the primary basis for the assignment of scores according to the ISONG Standards of Care (ISONG & ANA 1998) and Performance Indicators (GNCC 2003). Here the applicants describe their nursing practice, and the scorers must determine if the standards have been satisfactorily met. Each standard is broken into subcategories. The scorer then examines and analyzes each case study for inclusion of the components of the standard and the satisfactory performance of delivery of nursing care by the applicant. Below is an example of a score sheet the scorers use to measure a portion of the outcome identification standard.

After thorough review and analysis of each section of the portfolio, the scorer determines the level of competency the applicant demonstrates in each particular area. The applicant's practice level according to the documentation in the portfolio

---

The genetics advanced practice nurse provides consultation to the client and family, community, nurses, and/or other healthcare providers to enhance the plan of care and/or the abilities of others to provide appropriate care to individuals and families with genetic conditions.

STANDARD NUMBER	COMPONENTS OF STANDARD	INDICATORS OF SATISFACTORY ACCOMPLISHMENT	PERFORMANCE ASSESSMENT*
Vi-1	Provides consultation activities that promote health and facilitate management for persons or groups with or at risk for genetic condition(s).	a. Uses consultation models, interviewing and communication techniques, interdisciplinary teamwork. b. Uses problem-solving skills and change and system theories. c. Establishes working alliance with the client based on mutual respect and role responsibilities. d. Respects decision to implement care plan or system change remains the responsibility of the client. e. Ensures locus of control remains with client. f. Promotes health and facilitation of management of people or groups with or at risk for genetic conditions. g. Shows awareness and evidence of respect for confidentiality, ethical, legal, and social issues.	

*Score ranges from 4 to 10, with a score of 4–6 indicating that improvement is needed, 7 indicating a neutral assessment, 8 indicating that expectations have been met, and 9–10 indicating that expectations have been exceeded.

is evaluated to determine the extent to which his or her submission meets the *Statement on the Scope and Standards of Genetics Clinical Nursing Practice.*

Scorers may approach scoring in a manner that is most comfortable to them. They use the ISONG Standards, Performance Indicators, and the GNCC *Portfolio Evaluation and Scoring Training Manual* (selected content is included in Appendix C) to ensure consistency in comparing portfolio contents to the expected level of quality described in the training retreats. Guidelines are provided for the numerical assignment of each score. However, scorers are allowed some variability in their management of the scoring process. Some scorers are very precise, scoring each piece of a section to determine an overall average of a section. Other scorers have found it easier to get an overall "gestalt" impression of a section and the portfolio submission as a whole. No matter what the method of determining the scores, the most important factor is for each scorer to consistently apply the same scoring method to all the portfolios being scored. Following is an example of the score guide used for GNCC portfolios.

EVALUATION AREAS BASED UPON ISONG SCOPE AND STANDARDS FOR THE ADVANCE PRACTICE NURSE IN GENETICS   **SCORE***

Category 1: Evaluation of Client Care

Section 1: Assessment—The client and family affected by or at risk for a genetic condition are assessed by the genetics nurse to identify risk factors and interventions, information, service and referral needs.
  1) Collect comprehensive client information.
  2) Interpret comprehensive client information.

Section 2: Diagnosis—The genetics nurse determines diagnoses by analyzing assessment data consistent with the nurse's education and state nurse practice act.
  1) Derives diagnoses based on assessment data.

Section 3: Outcome Identification—The genetics nurse identifies expected outcomes individualized to the client.
  1) Derives measurable outcome from diagnosis.
  2) Outcomes are client sensitive.

Section 4: Planning—The genetics nurse develops a care plan with client, whenever possible, prescribing nursing interventions to attain expected outcomes.
  1) Develops comprehensive intervention plan tailored to client's genetic condition and healthcare need.

Section 5: Implementation—The genetics nurse implements interventions identified in the care plan.
  1) Implements plan.
  2) Identifies genetic risk factors among individual, family, and community.
  3) Provides client-centered health teaching.
  4) Coordinates health-related services for continuity of care from agencies.
  5) Promotes genetic health for client, family, and community.
  6) Provides genetic counseling and psychosocial support counseling.
  7) Uses therapeutic communication skills to assist client.
  8) Collaborates with other health professionals to facilitate client care.
  9) Provides consultation that facilitates management for persons or groups.

Section 6: Evaluation—The genetics nurse evaluates the progress of the client and family toward obtainment of outcomes.
  1) Engages in a systematized ongoing evaluation of client and family.
  2) Documents changes in assessment, diagnosis, and plan of care.

Evaluation Areas Based Upon ISONG Scope and Standards for the Advance Practice Nurse in Genetics	Score*

Category 2: Formal and Informal Education

1) RN license in good standing; other nursing certification(s), if applicable.

2) Genetic certification, if applicable.

3) Transcripts: Are the transcripts original? What is the range of course work and grades from both undergraduate and postgraduate education? Are courses related to genetics? That is: human genetics; molecular and biochemical genetics; ethical, legal, and social issues; clinical applications of genetics including genetic counseling; genetic variations in populations.

4) Continuing education: Continuing education must be undertaken within five years of application and be related to genetics. What is the quality of the continuing education? Are the contact hours from on-site courses, self-study programs from journals, computer-based media, or online training modules? Are they offered by a reputable agency, organization, or academic institution? Does the applicant demonstrate a commitment to improving his or her genetic knowledge base with a variety of topics (subject matter) in genetics applicable to his or her clinical practice area? Is there evidence of 50 contact hours of genetic continuing education? Are the continuing education contact hours from a single provider or a variety of providers?

Category 3: Teaching/Educational Efforts by the Applicant

Educational programs—Does the applicant show evidence (such as teaching plans, slide or overhead texts, other media descriptions or examples) of:
  Presentations and/or lectures at professional conferences?
  Presentations and/or lectures at worksite conferences?
  Courses in accredited schools and continuing education?
  Presentations/lectures at community events/conferences directed to patients and families, consumers, support groups, etc.?
  Web site, online, other media?
  Publications: hard copy required, abstract accepted if text more than 25 pages?
  Marketing materials: brochures, flyers showing applicant's contributions are acceptable?
  Summary letters of teaching provided, handouts from presentations?
  Slide handouts? (course/conference evaluation comments and ratings are valuable)
  Other documentation prepared by applicant?
  Evidence of patient, family and/or client teaching required for credential award? (evidence of education of consumers, community groups, and professionals is valuable)

Category 4: Other Achievements

Research activities (principal investigator, research team member).
Includes investigations conducted by the applicant alone or in cooperation with other investigators (research and scholarship may be funded or unfunded but must be verifiable by the Score Team).
Summaries, abstracts, abbreviated reports, listings of publications, and related materials are recognized as evidence.

Special recognitions.
Awards and honors.
Certificates, letters.

Source: Adapted from GNCC 2003.

*Score ranges from 4 to 10, with a score of 4–6 indicating that improvement is needed, 7 indicating a neutral assessment, 8 indicating that expectations have been met, and 9–10 indicating that expectations have been exceeded.

Use of retreats allows the Score Team to meet one or two times per year. The first retreat of the year is generally held in January to introduce new Score Team members. A sharing of the mission, philosophy, and historical perspectives of the Genetic Nursing Credentialing Commission and the unique use of portfolios for credentialing genetics nurse clinicians is presented. There is a business meeting, and intensive instruction of the scorers also occurs. The second retreat is held in July, after the scoring has taken place and the scores submitted to the Neural Net Software representatives from the Center for Self-Sustaining Leadership (CSL). Individual portfolios are reviewed. Significant issues or concerns are discussed (such as departures from the *Statement on the Scope and Standards of Genetics Clinical Nursing Practice*) and the score report is reviewed. The Score Team then makes a final credentialing decision. Each retreat is about 48 hours long, with Score Team members spending the entire time together.

A large portion of the January retreat training time is dedicated to familiarizing the new scorers with the standards of care set by the International Society of Nurses in Genetics (ISONG & ANA 1998). These core indicators are used by the Score Team to evaluate the clinical practice features of the portfolio. Also during this retreat, new Score Team members are instructed about the validity and reliability of the scoring process through the training sessions and use of neural net software. Scorers often will have initial impressions formed just as they begin to score a portfolio. For example, the actual presentation of the portfolio or the nurse's practice area may influence a scorer. The scorers are informed that the neural net software compensates for these human tendencies that reduce objectivity in the scoring process.

The importance of the in-person meeting with veteran scorers is significant. New problems and challenges (such as educational backgrounds or evidence of continuing education programs submitted by applicants) that appeared since the previous scoring rounds are reviewed and discussed. Anticipated challenges as well as possible solutions are also reviewed. These discussions integrate the new scorers into the team immediately. In both the January training retreat and the July scoring retreat, all attendees experience an open, accepting environment. All comments, questions, and criticisms are welcome. New ideas or observations are received openly. This provides a very positive, constructive, and effective working environment. Score debriefing retreats are discussed in more detail later in this chapter.

The *Portfolio Evaluation and Scoring Training Manual* supplies a significant portion of the preparation of new scorers as well as a continued reference for the veteran scorers. It serves to provide guidelines and reference points to the Score Team members, and it reflects the GNCC-established policies and procedures for the portfolio evaluation process. The manual was developed as a resource for all scorers.

The section "How to Grade the Portfolio" is the central part of the manual. These are the pages that are dog-eared and well worn during the first scoring round of portfolios for new scorers. Invaluable guidelines and suggestions from experienced scorers are contained in this section, including helpful hints such as "read and score portfolios as they come in; do not wait to read them all at once." Basics such as "make and keep notes regularly" are also included. There is also a list of what documents to have nearby, before the scorer starts the scoring process. Although the scoring process is presented in the January retreat, the manual provides a useful resource to the scorers once they begin the scoring process independently several months later. This

The *Portfolio Evaluation and Scoring Training Manual* contains the following information:

1 Timeline from training to the final retreat and recommending the credential
2 Guidelines and ethical standards
3 How to grade the portfolio
4 Neural net portfolio statistical analysis information
5 Glossary
6 Sample neural net software web site scoring pages
7 Genetic Nursing Credentialing Commission (GNCC) bylaws
8 GNCC Committee and Score Team members
9 Portfolio application guidelines
10 Samples of selected pages from previously submitted portfolios with reviewing scorers commentary

segment gives step-by-step instructions for scoring each section of the portfolio, including how to evaluate the applicant's curriculum vitae, education transcripts, and continuing education.

Another important part of the manual for the scorers is the section that contains sample documents from previous portfolio submissions. Sample case studies provide useful examples of high-quality work, as well as middle-range and low-quality work. These sample case studies also include multiple Score Team rater commentaries. Finally, important general advice such as the cross-checking of information throughout the scoring process is continually stressed throughout the scoring manual.

Debriefing the Score Team

The Score Team meets for a weekend retreat after all the scores have been given to the portfolios, in order to review and discuss individual aspects of scoring various sections of each portfolio. No scores are changed after the discussions during the retreat so as not to influence the validity of the process. It is done purely as a reflective process to learn how the other members of the team consider and arrive at scores for different sections of each portfolio submission.

During these debriefings many aspects of the portfolios are discussed. Portfolios are discussed as a whole, one at a time, with input from each team member according to their written notes. Portfolios are reviewed with respect to areas of particular strength and excellence, for example. Team members share the aspects of each portfolio that have been most impressive or outstanding to them, such as the quality or depth of the case studies, the applicant's clinical expertise, or educational achievements.

Even livelier discussions occur when the Score Team discovers missing, incorrect, ambiguous, or unethical items in the portfolios. For example, during one debriefing, there was found to be a breach of patient confidentiality in one of the case studies submitted. It is explicitly stated in the portfolio submission guidelines that patient confidentiality is to be protected at all times, and that personal information such as names, birth dates, and medical record numbers are to be removed so as not to identify the patient or family. The Score Team talked about the importance of patient confidentiality and whether the breach was significant enough to prevent the applicant from receiving the credential. After a thorough examination of the concerns and the portfolio in question, the Score Team concluded that the applicant could still be considered in good standing to receive the credential.

The quality of documentation, style of presentation of the case studies, and impressions of overall portfolio presentation are also reviewed. One interesting topic of discussion has been how well the applicants have followed instructions for assembling the portfolios. Very detailed and explicit directions for submitting the criteria for the portfolios are provided. There is an extensive application packet to be followed, (see Appendix B for sample pages from the *Applications Guidelines Packet*) as well as a final checklist (see below) for applicants to use before final submission of the portfolio. Despite these instructions, some items in some of the portfolios are not submitted according to the guidelines provided by the GNCC. The Score Team members have examined the contents of these portfolios against the instructions given and made decisions based on the evidence submitted.

Finally, after all the portfolios and scores are discussed, the team considers recommendations for improving the portfolio application process and changes to be made for the next cycle of portfolio applicants. Modifications to the *Application Guidelines Packet* for the Advanced Practice Nurse in Genetics and the Genetics Clinical Nurse are then approved by the GNCC leadership and distributed in the next credentialing cycle.

The preparation and education of Score Team members is a large part of the retreats, and they require quite a lot of energy and planning. However, through these training sessions, many constructive suggestions, exchanges of ideas, and changes have occurred. The content of the training manual as well as the training process itself is a "work in progress" that allows each new Score Team to bring fresh insights and ideas to the project. For example, changes to the various forms used in the portfolios have continually been made to simplify the application, as well as the scoring, process. The welcoming of new members' ideas is of great importance to the success of this process.

Guidelines and Ethical Standards

The GNCC Score Team acts in good faith to evaluate portfolios submitted in a fair way and to provide ratings that are commensurate with the *Statement on the Scope and Standards of Genetics Clinical Nursing Practice*. The integrity of the portfolio evaluation and scoring process as well as the protection and respect due to the individual credential applicants are emphasized to all Score Team members. All written notes or documents and discussions of portfolio evaluation and scoring are kept confidential. No Score Team members may disclose any part of a portfolio application contents to anyone other than other Score Team members, leaders, or GNCC officers. In addition, Score Team attentiveness to privacy and confidentiality principles is imperative for the applicant as well as his or her clients their families.

CHECKLIST FOR THE APNG PORTFOLIO—ORIGINAL CONTENTS

Sections of Portfolio should be labeled on tabs in notebook binder as listed below. Corresponding materials
Must be placed behind each tab. This checklist should be used as Portfolio cover sheet in front of the first tab

Applicant Initials	Tab	Requirement	Comments
		FOUR ADDITIONAL COPIES WILL BE STAPLED AND PLACED IN THE NOTEBOOK POCKETS	
	Top of Port-folio	**Application cover** form with applicant information, signature and notary public signature and seal	
	1.	**Proof of RN license** in good standing and **Nonrefundable Money Order or Cashier's Check** for $400 application fee made out to GNCC, INC. for ISONG members, $550 for non-ISONG members	
	2.	**Curriculum Vitae**	See CV Standard form; recommended components
	3.	**Letter of verification from Employer, Supervisor, or Professional Colleague**; verifies that applicant has provided care to clients named in Log and/or Case Studies—must be sealed in envelope with signature on flap	See Standard Forms section Letter of verification must be on organization or agency letterhead OF THE THREE KINDS OF DOCUMENTS (Letter of Verification, Performance Appraisal, and Peer Review) AT LEAST ONE MUST BE FROM A GENETIC HEALTH PROFESSIONAL, i.e. MD/PhD geneticist, CGC, APNG, or doctorally prepared nurse with training in genetics.
	4.	**Professional Performance Verification & Evaluation** form—must be sealed in envelope with signature on flap **Three Peer Reviews**—must be sealed in envelope with signature on flap	See Standard Forms section; Professional Performance Verification & Evaluation form for Employer, Supervisor, or Professional Colleague; Professional Performance Verification & Evaluation form for Peers
	5.	**Official transcripts** in sealed envelopes for all applicable undergraduate and graduate education programs (BSN required; Masters in Nursing or related field required in 2005 credentialing cycle) **Continuing Education certificates** and/or proof of attendance at applicable continuing education programs (minimum of 50 contact hours in the past 5 years)	Duplicated copies of Continuing Education Programs are acceptable. The Continuing Education materials must specify topic areas of genetics in the program. All documents are subject to verification by the GNCC, INC. Score Team members.
	6.	**50 Case Log** with verification signature of Supervisor or Professional Colleague for log required (use form); cases within 5 years of application	See form for Case Log with indications of ISONG Standards of Care See form for verification signature of Supervisor or Professional Colleague
	7.	**4 Case Studies** (taken from cases in Case Log) illustrating clinical practice that reflects the ISONG Standards of Care (see International Society of Nurses in Genetics, Inc. & American Nurses Association. (1998). <u>Statement on the scope and standards of genetics clinical nursing practice</u>. Washington, DC: American Nurses Publishing).	See Case Studies Guideline, recommended components; See example Case Study, Performance Indicators grading form and ratings given to example Case Study. This example is intended for applicant guidance
	8.	Appendices: Education and Other sections (teaching materials, research summaries, abstracts, publications, awards, recognitions, etc.)	This section may include copies and/or summaries of educational and research materials authored by the applicant. All documents are subject to verification by the GNCC, Inc. Score Team.

All Score Team members are informed of the applicant's right to due process. "Due process will consist of a) written request for review of the Score Team evaluations and reason(s) for review directed to the officers of the GNCC; b) review of the portfolio contents, the evaluation and scoring records, and other pertinent materials by an impartial panel assembled from within the GNCC (i.e., an alternate Score Team trained in evaluation and scoring procedures); and c) written response to the request from the officers of the GNCC. Legal consultants will be used if/when resolution of review cannot be achieved by either the GNCC or the individual applicant" (Monsen in 2003, p. 4).

Individual scorers must keep meticulous logs of comments and scoring criteria for each individual portfolio that is scored, in order to ensure ease of auditing and accuracy of findings. In order to maintain the integrity of the scoring process, all scoring is performed independently, and any consulting regarding specific portfolios is forbidden until each Score Team member enters all scores. A communication blackout of sorts is instituted, and no scorers may communicate with other Score Team members at any time during the scoring process. All scores must be submitted by the deadline, and portfolios are discussed at the retreat in July. Neither the applicant's overall individual score nor the scores determined by the scorer for each specific area are ever revealed. After scoring is completed, all portfolio submissions are returned to the central distribution center and all copies are shredded.

Summary

The training of the GNCC Score Teams rests upon the explicit guidelines (see examples in Appendix C) for evaluation of portfolios and entails on-site retreats as well as Score Team member individual study and commitment to fairly appraising the applicant's submissions for the APNG and GCN credentials. Score Teams include clinicians, educators, and nurses in related roles with a breath of experience in genetics health care as well as nursing education. The portfolio scoring system covers several areas or categories of content, all of which are based upon the *Statement on the Scope and Standards of Genetics Clinical Nursing Practice.*

References

Genetic Nursing Credentialing Commission (GNCC). (2003). *Portfolio evaluation and scoring training manual.* Hot Springs, AR: Author.

International Society of Nurses in Genetics (ISONG) & American Nurses Association (ANA). (1998). *Statement on the scope and standards of genetics clinical nursing practice.* Washington, DC: ANA.

Use of Neural Net Technology to Quantify Portfolio Evaluations

7

Dave Holmes
Robert McAlpine
Jack Russell

Well-defined, inclusive, and user-friendly standards, components of standards, performance indicators, and a scoring system, along with well-trained and highly competent evaluators are essential elements for a reliable portfolio credentialing system. Satisfactorily developing these elements requires expertise, patience, and collaboration with the nursing specialty organization.

When the chairperson of the GNCC, a commission established by the International Society of Nurses of Genetics (ISONG), approached the Center for Self-Sustaining Leadership (CSL) for assistance in developing their portfolio process, she noted that their members had already spent considerable time designing the requirements based upon the *Statement on the Scope and Standards of Genetics Clinical Nursing Practice* of ISONG and the American Nurses Association (ANA) (1998). This included a comprehensive series of standards and measurement criteria in accordance with the ANA's template of standards for recognized nursing specialties. At the time of the initial consultation, we noted that the standards were not in a format that was user-friendly to potential portfolio applicants and evaluators, nor was their measurement easily identified. The group was struggling, and the committee needed our immediate help. The chairperson also clearly communicated that the final evaluation of each portfolio had to be valid and consistent.

It was the beginning of a collaborative and productive relationship between two groups with different but essential expertise that resulted in what we view as a valid and consistent evaluation process for a performance-based portfolio. The GNCC commission members represented both academia and clinical practice in genetics. They were highly qualified, with extensive knowledge and experience in their field. On the other hand, the CSL team had no experience in nursing or genetics. However, they brought to the effort extensive practical experience and knowledge on the development and implementation of performance-based standards, quantifiable measurements of portfolio components, and the application of a neural net program to ensure evaluator consistency (reliability). Combining different expertise was a professionally gratifying experience for all and, perhaps more important, accomplished the goals effectively. These goals included:

1. Satisfying the ISONG membership's directive to develop an advanced practitioner of genetics nursing credential based on a performance-based portfolio process that would be recognized by its members, the nursing profession, other healthcare professions, regulatory agencies, and (potentially) third-party payers as meeting high standards.
2. Assessing applicants' clinical performance.
3. Making the process affordable, understandable, and achievable for applicants and the GNCC.
4. Ensuring that the process is
   - user friendly for applicants, evaluators, and administrators;
   - structured to respect confidentiality of applicants and evaluators;
   - consistent and valid.

Development Process

The portfolio development process begins by identifying a professional level of competency. "Level" is the relative position along a professional career pathway that a person has or can attain. Often the members of a profession recognize a person's attainment of each level by awarding a credential, degree, or certificate. For instance, in nursing there is a series of educational levels beginning with entry-level technical education (for example, the practical or vocational nursing programs) and ending with advanced academic achievement (doctoral and postdoctoral education). These education levels do not necessarily encompass all of the clinical skills required of advanced practitioners in various specialization fields, such as genetics. The members of ISONG recognized the need for a professional credential and had explored certification or credentialing comparable to those held by colleagues in genetics. In 1999, they appointed a task force to accomplish this task knowing that the public, other health professionals, and third-party payers needed awareness of and confidence in the unique expertise of genetics nurses. Credentialing would help achieve this recognition.

GNCC members started by identifying generalist and advanced levels of genetics nursing practice. These two levels are based on education, experience, focus of nursing practice, specific clinical roles, and professional functions. The basic differences between the two "are the complexity of decision making, leadership, the ability to negotiate complex organizations, and expanded practice skills and knowledge in nursing and genetics" (ISONG & ANA 1998, p. 6). The generalist level requires an applicant to have completed a baccalaureate degree in nursing and have an RN license. The advanced level requires a master's in nursing or equivalent, an RN license, and clinical responsibilities for genetic counseling. (Additional requirements are discussed in

Chapters 5 and 6, and at the GNCC web site, www.geneticnurse.org). The members of the GNCC, at the same time, recognized that any definition of genetics nursing practice that differentiated between the generalist and advanced levels would, of necessity, have to be congruent with legal parameters, policies, and ethical codes of conduct prescribed by regulatory authorities and licensing bodies in the United States (and internationally, in view of possible future opportunities for genetics nursing credentialing in other countries).

Standards, Components of Standards, and Indicators of Satisfactory Accomplishment

The process of molding standards, components of standards, and indicators of satisfactory performance is challenging to members and leaders of a profession. It is like giving a group of artists a hunk of marble, a list of criteria, and the task of sculpting them together. In CSL's experience, certain principles help guide the sculpting process:

1. Create a series of pyramids with a standard being at the pinnacle of each one. Components of standards form the next level and performance indicators constitute the foundation level.
2. Write standards, components, and indicators as declarative phrases or sentences. Keep them simple and user-friendly! Each level forms the building blocks that clarifies and supports the one above it.
3. Avoid using broad, general terms such as "appropriate," "comprehensive," or "successful." They are too ambiguous and subjective. For instance, having a standard that states, "The nurse will take appropriate actions" does not provide a clear indication of specific actions. What is appropriate to one person may not be to another. However, if any of these terms or similar ones are used, ensure that the next level clarifies it.

From CSL's perspective, standards define the minimal performance, education, and experience expected of a person at a certain level. We can think of standards as a "bar" or hurdle that a person must clear in order to qualify for a credential. A professional group awards credentials on the basis of applicants achieving standards, whether by exams, observed performance, or other forms of documentation. It is therefore essential that these standards be clearly and fully defined.

During the defining phase, standards are identified as either screening and/or evaluative. Some are solely screening, some are both screening and evaluative, and some are solely evaluative ones. For instance, an applicant must meet the GNCC's portfolio screening standards, which include (among other elements) proof of a valid registered nurse (RN) license in good standing, a curriculum vitae, and a log of 50 cases. A screening criterion is an all-or-nothing proposition. The required element is present or it is not. An administrator reviews a submitted portfolio and determines if it includes these items. If it does, then it has met the screening standards and can proceed to the evaluative phase. If it does not, then it is rejected and returned to the applicant.

The requirement of four case studies is a screening and evaluative standard. Once the administrator verifies that a portfolio includes four case studies, she or he passes it along to reviewers (evaluators; the Score Team, for example, at the GNCC) who then read, assess, and score it. Other standards are strictly evaluative, such as "The genetics nurse develops a plan of care that prescribes nursing interventions to attain expected outcomes" (ISONG & ANA 1998, p. 13). Again, these are the ones that evaluators read, assess, and score.

Components of standards are critical tasks. They are explicit and implied activities that a person must accomplish in order to satisfy a standard that they support. For instance, the ISONG portfolio has a standard, "The client and the family affected by or at risk for a genetic condition are assessed by the genetics nurse to identify risk factors and intervention, information, service, and referral needs" (ISONG & ANA 1998, p. 9). This standard implies scientific and technological competencies, knowledge, and expertise (general academic as well as nursing subjects, areas specific to genetics, and clinical issues. It illustrates a "holistic" approach. The GNCC task force wrote two explicit critical tasks that clarify the standard (GNCC 2003): "I-1: Collect comprehensive client information." This task addresses the first portion of the standard, which requires assessment. "I-2: Interpret comprehensive client information." This addresses the second portion, which identifies an action to be taken to identify risks and determine needs. Once the nurse has gathered information, she or he must make sense of it in regard to the best actions for the affected client and family. The applicant must successfully demonstrate that she or he consistently satisfies these tasks. They are essential. The applicant can do more, but not less, in order to meet the "bar" or standard.

Indicators of satisfactory accomplishment, or performance indicators, provide answers to another challenge. How does an applicant know if she or he has shown sufficient evidence for the various activities associated with a critical task? How does an evaluator know? Performance indicators define those actions that an applicant must complete, often in a prescribed manner, to meet each critical task and satisfy an evaluator. They also expand upon and clarify the critical tasks. The above-mentioned first critical task has 17 such indicators (see Standard I: Assessment; I-1 Performance Indicator, in Chapter 5). The fifth one states, "History in standard pedigree formats for at least three generations." It is assumed that an applicant at this level understands "standard pedigree formats" and must show this format for a minimum of three generations. Under the second critical task are 17 indicators (see following page). Therefore, an applicant must show evidence that she or he has successfully accomplished each of these 34 indicators in order to meet the two components of the standard, which in turn support the one standard.

	STANDARD I	
	Assessment	
	The client and the family affected by or at risk for a genetic condition are assessed by the genetics nurse to identify risk factors and intervention, information, service, and referral needs.	

	PERFORMANCE INDICATOR	CHARACTERISTIC COMPONENTS EXPECTED IN CASE STUDY TEXTS
I-2	Interpret comprehensive client information	1. Biophysical status using dysmorphology examination (assessment of abnormal physical features, if present)/genetic testing results and routine laboratory tests. 2. Coping and adaptation patterns by patient and/or family. 3. Cultural, community, and family support systems. 4. Economic, environmental, and health policy factors affecting health status. 5. Family history in standard pedigree format for at least three generations. 6. Medical history inclusive but not limited to prenatal, perinatal, and neonatal histories as appropriate. 7. Family integrity, structure, and level of functioning. 8. Growth and development status. 9. Health beliefs and practices of patient and/or family. 10. Psychological, spiritual, values, and beliefs status. 11. Strengths of individual patient and/or family. 12. Risk factors associated with genetic conditions or birth defects. 13. Include health-related goals, roles, and responsibilities in discussion. 14. Discuss data assessment and analysis with client and family. 15. Identify patient's and/or family's expectations and needs for care and education. 16. Considers ethical, legal, and social issues. 17. Documents information in standard format (for example, the use of assessment terms and narrative format commonly accepted in healthcare settings).

Source: ISONG & ANA 1998, p. 9.

While establishing standards is a necessary first step, defining components of standards and performance indicators of satisfactory accomplishment is often more challenging for groups. The professional experts must strike a balance between the abstract ideals of clinical practice and the portfolio contents to be scored by evaluators. The CSL team has found that working through this process is difficult and most groups struggle with the challenge of deriving performance indicators from standards of practice.

In the case of the GNCC. CSL facilitated the process of defining expert practice in genetics nursing by guiding the nurse experts as they worked to translate the ANA and ISONG standards into observable and measurable components of standards and performance indicators. The GNCC expert group included both academicians and clinicians who were able to bring considerable experience with constructing measurable outcomes to capturing and defining expertise in advance practice nursing. After this phase of developing components of standards and performance indicators was completed, the GNCC core group agreed that they met their goals for defining the elements of practice and characteristics of a successful advances practice genetics nurse clinician.

Scoring

As evaluators (reviewer or GNCC Score Team member) work their way through each portfolio section, they arrive at conclusions as to whether or not an applicant has met evaluative standards. They compare the written documentation with performance indicators and draw conclusions that are then translated into quantified scores. Each evaluator submits her or his scores at a CSL secure web site. In CSL's experience, there are a number of valid rating systems. Some are pass/fail or go/no-go. Some use numbers or letters on a Likert like scale (low to high relative value scale; for example, very strong, strong, adequate, weak, and very weak). We chose to use whole-number inclinations of 2 as in 4, 6, 8, and 10. We applied them to the following performance levels:

10 = Exceeds Standard
 8 = Meets Standard
 7 = Neutral
 6 = Needs Improvement
 4 = Needs Much Improvement

We randomly chose 8 as a number to equate with meeting standards. We could have easily used letters like S = Standard. The key is to attempt to pick numbers or letters that elicit little, if any, emotional response from applicants or evaluators. For instance, A, B, and C or 60, 70, 80, or 90 are not used because they are too closely associated with school and other arenas where ratings of performance occur. People often comment that they find it difficult to differentiate between two sequential, whole numbers in a rating scale, such as between 4 and 5. We addressed this by using even number such as 4, 6, 8 and 10. We have found that evaluators have no trouble differentiating between 8 (meets standard) and 10 (exceeds standard), or 4 (needs much improvement) and 6 (needs improvement). Occasionally they do have a problem differentiating between 6 (needs improvement) and 8 (meets standard), most likely because now they are at a critical juncture of making a decision about an applicant meeting or not meeting a standard and the possibility of not passing. Does the applicant meet or pass the "bar"? Also, they may believe that they do not have the expertise in a particular area to make a sound judgment. If an evaluator scored an item with a 7, the scoring program read this as a neutral item, and it had no bearing on the final rating.

Reviewers

Qualified and carefully chosen reviewers or evaluators are essential to the credibility of the portfolio system. Thorough training helps to ensure the validity of their judgments as a group. Each portfolio must be assigned to a person who has the experience, knowledge, and ability to evaluate the portfolio. We have had situations where evaluators experienced difficulty making a "yes" or "no" judgment. A number of reasons were given, such as not feeling qualified to make a decision regarding a particular standard or just not being able to decide. Initially, we made allowances through the neural net program without compromising the final results by having a neutral score. However, we have come to the conclusion that it is unacceptable for an evaluator to use the 7 (neutral) rating in regard to specific component of standards. The evaluators must be qualified and willing to judge each portion of a portfolio. It is a systems challenge to ensure that each portfolio is assigned to evaluators who are competent and able to assess all of it.

How many evaluators are sufficient? The CSL and GNCC teams decided on five. Three could do the job. More than three strengthens the reliability and validity of the process. An odd number of evaluators, such as five, can help avoid a tie. Having more than three also provides a safety cushion in case one or two evaluators at the last moment are not able to fulfill their scoring duties. This is not to say that a group should not have more than five, but there should be some strong reasons to do so. If there are more than five, the process becomes cumbersome.

A balance is needed among identifying, training, and maintaining a sufficient number of qualified evaluators, anticipating the number of submitted portfolios, and determining costs. To date, the CSL and GNCC negotiated a service contract that includes payment for technical consultation, management of neural net technology in portfolio score calculations, and follow-up evaluation of score pattern reports (averaging approximately $50 annually per applicant; this is after completion of the initial consultation, web site design, and setup work). The Score Team training process needs to be thoroughly thought out to include practical administrative details, training materials, sharing of lessons learned from previous evaluators, conversations regarding standards, components and indicators, process fine-tuning, and a method for resolving philosophical questions (for example, "Does this address cultural diversity?").

The GNCC group has found that it takes an evaluator or reviewer who has experience grading and/or editing papers approximately one to two hours to complete one portfolio. For less experienced evaluators or when problems arise, it can take three hours or more. This information helps determine the number of portfolios an evaluator can realistically and effectively score, and the required number of evaluators. The group decided not to pay evaluators. However, it is a factor that may be reconsidered in the future. All of this involves a bottom-line cost that should be identified and included, at least somewhat, in the applicant's fee.

GNCC evaluators participate for a minimum of three years. The first year they are "interns." They go through the entire scoring process but their scores do not determine a "go" or "no-go" (pass or fail) for applicants. Their scores are checked for internal consistency with each other and with the more experienced evaluators, whose scores determine the actual results by the neural net program after score entry on the secure web site. Evaluators meet once or twice each year for in-person discussions, which may or may not be necessary for other groups. During the first meeting, the experienced evaluators introduce and lead the new group through the process and share their experiences—how long does it take to read and score a portfolio, don't do them all at one sitting, how to score and enter scores on the program, etc. They meet a second time after they all have submitted their scores. This enables them to review what occurred, what went well, and what needs to be changed. The "interns" now become the reviewers whose scores are critical.

Evaluators read and score each portfolio. They cannot converse among themselves once they receive portfolios until the process is completed to protect from biasing the scores of other Score Team members. This helps prevent one person or a group from influencing others in regards to particular portfolios. However, there is an exception. If a philosophical question or issue (for example, variation in healthcare process from facility to facility) arises while reading a portfolio that may pertain to all of them, the evaluator is encouraged to bring it to the attention of the Score Team administrator (the GNCC president) for discussion. A decision is made about applicability to all of the portfolios, even if it means rescoring, and the Score Team members are directed to proceed to ensure the integrity of the scoring process. To date, such a philosophical question has not arisen that necessitated reentry of scores.

CSL has created a secure, user-friendly web page dedicated solely to the management of the GNCC's portfolio scores. Entering them is simple and takes perhaps a minute or two to complete. A designated CSL person receives the scores and puts them through a neural net "pattern recognition" program. If an "outlier" score shows up, the administrator is notified and asks the evaluators to review and score that particular section or standard and resubmit all of the scores. If it happens again, then CSL facilitates a discussion focusing on the section or standard in question. To date we have not had to go back to evaluators for a review. However, there have been situations where one evaluator's scores did not pass an individual while others did. A discussion occurred among the evaluators, and they were able to arrive at consensus. The group made the decision and not the program.

Neural Net (Pattern Recognition) Scoring Program

The use of a neural net program, often referred to as a "pattern recognition" or "artificial intelligence" program, has gained wide acceptance and diverse applications in many health service professions (Hanson & Marshall 2001). It attempts to duplicate the nonlinear process (back-and-forth reasoning, circular and "out-of-the box" thinking) that people use to arrive at most daily conclusions, but unlike people, it does not forget information. In regards to the GNCC portfolio, it is used to determine consistency of evaluator scoring and to make an initial determination if an applicant has met the standards based on submitted scores. It is essential to remember that ultimately the evaluators, and not a computer program, make the final decision. Why use a neural net program?

1. It is highly accurate—an approximately 98% accuracy rate has been found with cumulative, overall GNCC scoring patterns to date.
2. Each portfolio score entered by an evaluator is compared with a similar component of standard scores previously entered. These include scores from previous years and current ones. This ensures that each portfolio is evaluated with the same methods as previous portfolios and ensures consistency of scoring (promotes reliability in portfolio evaluation).
3. If, in the future, scored items are added or removed from the portfolio, or if the standards change, the neural net can still apply historical data by comparing the past with the present.

It is not our purpose nor are we fully qualified to present a thorough explanation of how a neural net program works. We explored using a traditional statistical model and one using a neural net. The challenge was to find a mathematical-based model that could reliably accept subjective, quantifiable evaluation data from different sources and potentially changing evaluation criteria and arrive at highly predictable results (98%). A neural net program easily meets this challenge by offering a different paradigm for computing data. Simply stated, the program compares entered data or scores to historical data within defined, programmed parameters. This continues until a pattern emerges. The neural net recognizes this pattern and applies it to the portfolio and evaluator. It sets the "bar" that each portfolio and evaluator must meet to be successful. It also identifies those scores or evaluators that do not meet the "bar" (consultation with neural net authority at Ward Systems Group, Inc., Executive Park West, 5 Hillcrest Dr., Frederick, MD 21703, www.wardsystems.com).

The nursing profession reflects an ongoing debate about competency found in many professions, especially education, throughout the country. How does a profession adequately determine if an applicant has met credentialing standards? How does it determine if a person can do the job expected by the public, the healthcare profession and third-party payers? For decades written tests have been used to determine this. If an applicant has the knowledge to respond accurately to a series of questions and the questions reflect what a person should know at a particular level, then the assumption is that she or he is qualified. However, in order to be successful, a person must retain specific knowledge and learn how to take a specific type of test. Templates or computers are used to score tests that have specified answers for each question. The final score determines a pass/fail outcome. People are not needed for these decisions because the process is theoretically objective and straightforward. The exams are objective only because answers are well defined and easily recognizable, such as "true" or "false" or other specific words, phrases, figures, and/or equations. On the other hand, standards and associated questions and answers may be objective, but the process of determining whether a person is meeting them is subjective, even though a large number of qualified individuals within a profession agree on the content of the standards.

There is an abundance of circumstantial evidence and increasing amount of research that indicates that tests often discriminate against applicants who may otherwise be qualified (for example, when an applicant has a testing disability). Moreover, examinations do not necessarily ensure clinical competency. For instance, standardized tests may require a person to apply theory to written clinical applications. Some individuals, for a variety of reasons, may find this extremely difficult but can easily do it when faced with real, everyday situations. Others have learned and are adapt at taking written tests but cannot consistently meet standards when faced with the pressures of applying theory in clinical situations.

When we add essay questions to tests, we increasingly add a modicum of subjectivity. An evaluator will have to read the answer and make a judgment as to its quality (correct and complete). This process is subjective within the accepted boundaries of a profession and based upon the knowledge, skills, and experience of an expert reviewer or evaluator. It is also why training of reviewers is essential. Two individuals may read the same material and arrive at slightly different judgments. Are both of these judgments valid, especially when awarding credentials? Yes, if the judgments are made within explicitly stated, well-defined boundaries. The portfolio process establishes these boundaries by defining standards, critical tasks, and indicators, and by training highly qualified evaluators. The GNCC portfolio requires four case studies. Evaluators apply a number of standards, critical tasks, and indicators to assess each lengthy case study.

However, the time comes when each evaluator must make the call and arrive at a judgment; some might call it a moment the evidence creates an impression of the applicant's qualifications. "Does the applicant have what it takes and has she or he adequately proven it? Can the applicant consistently meet standards in clinical practice based on my comparing presented evidence to our defined standards, critical tasks, and indicators?" It is a judgment based on the presented information and years of experience on the part of the evaluators. It is a qualitative, subjective judgment, made within consciously and professionally defined boundaries that increases its objectivity. By the same token, valid and acceptable differences of professional interpretations exist among evaluators. The pattern recognition program works extremely well with these subjective judgments and differences, and ensures that the final evaluations are consistent.

One might ask the question, "How is a neural net different from a statistical model?" Statistical models attempts to "curve-fit" data. If the data is linear or near-linear, it is likely to fit along a curve and is generated from the same objective source, in which case a statistical model would work fine. However, subjective data is nonlinear. Every portfolio differs, in some measure, from every other in terms of the clinical practice characteristics and the experience of the applicants. Evaluators come and go and each brings a different grading style, clinical and academic experience, weight of importance of standards, and personal standards for making judgments about evidence. This generates very different data from different subjective sources at different times, and these by their nature do not easily fit a linear, objective statistical model. Instead the data is fluid, chaotic (not linear or necessarily fitting a curve), and multidimensional, having objective standards and subjective experiences and judgments. The neural net program is purposely designed to accommodate nonlinear, multidimensional data to accept new inputs, learn from past data, and recognize emergent patterns. It serves to enhance, not replace, reviewers' conclusions.

The final scores are translated into a report and sent to the portfolio administrator, who shares it with reviewers. If the report highlights an applicant who did not meet standards, the group can then choose to enter into a discussion and arrive at a final decision. The report also highlights scores of an evaluator that are outliers compared to those of the others. For instance, one evaluator may score a particular component a 4 when the others gave scores of 8s and 10s. As discussed earlier, a process exists for resolving this type of situation.

Some individuals involved in certification or credentialing have challenged the portfolio process as too time-consuming and labor intensive for both applicants and evaluators. Could we effectively handle a large number of portfolios, say several hundred, a year? The simple answer is yes, especially if applicants can obtain information and submit their portfolios over the Internet, and align their documented knowledge and clinical experience to portfolio requirements over time. It is a systems challenge, especially in regard to the required number of evaluators, and pattern recognition can play an essential role beyond its current application. We can use it for initial screening of portfolios and scoring of subjective data, such as case studies. It is already being used in education to identify writing, reading comprehension, and mathematical levels. However, it is essential to remember that any use of a pattern recognition program is part of a comprehensive system and that qualified people must always make the final decisions. The use of a neural net program is the final stage of a process designed to ensure validity and consistency. It is an extremely powerful and flexible program that is dramatically changing how we determine professional, clinical competency. The GNCC's use of it is a solid beginning in exploring its potential application.

Summary

The GNCC has taken a portfolio system approach in awarding generalist and advanced nurse practice credentials to its qualified members, which in our opinion is applicable to other nursing specialties and healthcare professions. The system is designed to consistently assess applicants' abilities to perform at a clearly delineated professional clinical level. It is essential that each element of the system—standards, components of standards, performance indicators of satisfactory accomplishment, evaluators, and scoring method—be carefully defined, qualified, and integrated. Quality assurance at each stage is essential! In the end, the GNCC portfolio system has accomplished the goals outlined by the ISONG membership.

References

Genetic Nursing Credentialing Commission (GNCC). (2003). *Application Guidelines Packet*. Hot Springs, AR: Author.

Hanson, C. W., & Marshall, B. E. (2001). Artificial intelligence applications in the intensive care unit. *Critical Care Medicine, 29*, 427–435.

International Society of Nurses in Genetics (ISONG) & American Nurses Association (ANA). (1998). *Statement on the scope and standards of genetics clinical nursing practice*. Washington, DC: ANA.

Case Studies in Genetics Nursing 8

Rita Black Monsen, DSN, MPH, RN, FAAN

We have included three examples of case studies that were submitted in portfolios for the Advanced Practice Nurse in Genetics (APNG) credential with the Genetic Nursing Credentialing Commission (GNCC) to illustrate the kinds of narratives that come from clinician's practices. Each of the nurses who submitted case studies had the GNCC Application Guidelines Packet available to aid in composing the texts. You will see, in these illustrative case studies, that they all included the basic elements of standard documentation in the health professions—subjective data, objective data, assessment, plan, intervention, and evaluation (SOAPIE)—to some degree in their descriptions of nursing care. Their portfolio submissions included all of the required elements (and more) for the APNG credential.

Also, you will note that we have modified the identities and the patterns of health and illness of the patients and their families to protect their confidentiality. In addition, we have included illustrations of pedigree form of notation of family history in each case study (standard practice in genetic healthcare services). An example guide for pedigree symbols appears on the following page for those readers who are unfamiliar with the symbols used in delivery of genetic healthcare services. In addition, each case study will briefly discuss the meaning of the case and its implications for clinical nursing practice. Readers may wish to seek further information and resource materials for the clinical conditions discussed, which are available online at the web sites of the National Coalition for Health Professional Education in Genetics (www.nchpeg.org), the National Human Genome Research Institute (www.nhgri.nih.gov), and GeneTests (www.genetests.org), a web site funded by the National Institutes of Health that provides information about health conditions with a genetic component, educational resources, and listings of health professionals in genetics.

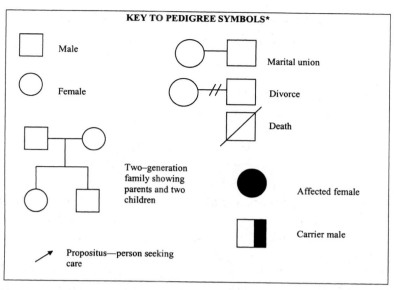

KEY TO PEDIGREE SYMBOLS*

Male

Female

Marital union

Divorce

Death

Two–generation family showing parents and two children

Affected female

Carrier male

Propositus—person seeking care

*The basic elements of the pedigree include those depicted above; fuller explanations of pedigree construction may be found in nursing and related health literature. Two suggested references are works by Bennett (1999) and Spahis (2002). In this figure, the symbol for the affected person is accompanied by a brief explanation of condition, usually a medical diagnosis. The symbol for the carrier person (above example is a heterozygote, or person with one copy of a genetic mutation) may be accompanied by an explanation of condition or carrier status.

References

Bennett, R. L. (1999). *The practical guide to the genetic family history*. New York: Wiley-Liss.

Spahis, J. (2002). Human genetics: Constructing a family pedigree. *American Journal of Nursing, 102*, 44–50.

Cancer Risk Assessment Case Study
Sue Miller-Samuel, MSN, RN, APNG

Dates of Care
Mid-September, early November

History/Past Medical History
This 47-year-old Caucasian female was referred to me for genetic risk assessment and counseling by her breast surgeon in light of her diagnosis at age 43 of invasive lobular metastatic breast cancer (premenopausal), and the fact she is of Eastern European descent. (Based upon the experience of several cancer risk programs in the United States, it is a well-accepted fact that the Ashkenazi Jewish population from Eastern Europe has an increased risk of heritable breast and ovarian cancers.) Based upon this information and the family history pattern explained below, this woman and her family qualified for Cancer Risk Assessment at our center. The consultand was treated with lumpectomy, radiation, and chemotherapy in the late 1990s. She subsequently became menopausal after her treatment and now has a severe case of osteoporosis documented on diagnostic workup. The consultand was mailed an initial intake packet for the Cancer Center after our initial phone conversation in mid-September.

Family History
The consultand's family history is significant for her mother being diagnosed with lung cancer in her 60s. Her mother died from aplastic anemia secondary to her cardiac medications. Her maternal grandfather was diagnosed with leukemia (type unknown) at age 75 and succumbed to the disease within one year. This grandfather worked as a tailor, and his exposure to chemicals is uncertain. (While the literature remains somewhat controversial regarding chemical exposures, chromosomal damage and subsequent cancers, the type of exposure may help evaluate the importance of a cancer occurrence in a given family. This can provide helpful information when doing pedigree analysis, utilizing mutation probability models, and providing risk assessment.) Paternal family history, while a bit sketchy, is noncontributory for cancer or potential cancer syndromes as reported.

The consultand presents as a reliable source. The physician collaborating with me on this family's genetic care agrees with this assessment.

Maternal Family History
Ethnicity: Eastern Europe
Mother: Significant history for lung cancer diagnosed in her 60s. The consultand's mother was a lifelong "regular" smoker. Maternal grandfather diagnosed with leukemia at 75; died that same year from leukemia. Of note is the fact that all of the consultand's maternal great-aunts (individuals labeled II:4 on the pedigree on the following page), and her maternal grandmother (II:2), are reported to have died under age 40, but the causes of their deaths are unknown.

Paternal Family History

Ethnicity: Eastern Europe

Father: Age 73 and suffered a myocardial infarction when he was 51 and had a four-vessel coronary artery bypass graft. Other paternal family history is noncontributory for cancer or potential cancer syndromes. However, we do not have the complete story because there is some intrafamilial estrangement (individuals III:5; III:6; II:5; II:6) or lack of family history that makes this information less than definitive.

Three-Generation Pedigree

See below.

Surgical History

1999: Left breast lumpectomy

GYN History

Menarche at age 14, gravida 2/ para 2. Regular periods until age 43 after chemotherapy. The consultand denies any hormone usage including birth control pills (as a source of exogenous estrogen, this might have had a bearing on development of breast cancer). Endometrial biopsy was done this year secondary to postmenopausal bleeding. The pathology findings revealed a fragment of a uterine polyp.

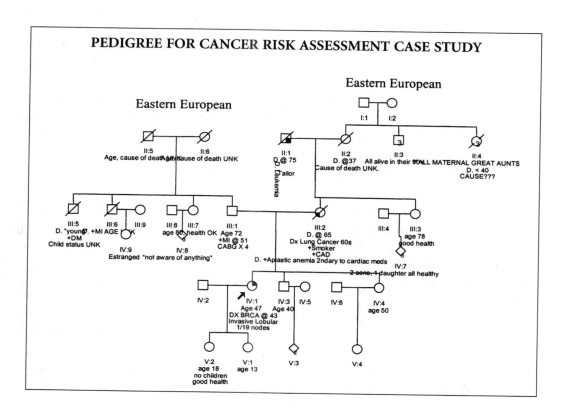

PEDIGREE FOR CANCER RISK ASSESSMENT CASE STUDY

Social History

This is a married woman who lives with her husband and two daughters ages 18 and 13. She has a professional career outside of the home. She denies current use of alcohol, tobacco, or recreational drugs. She did smoke one pack of cigarettes/week from ages 15 to 25.

Subjective Data

The consultand has requested a genetic counseling session in light of her premenopausal breast cancer diagnosis and her Eastern European heritage. At our counseling appointment in November, the consultand presents as pleasant, articulate, and well informed on her breast cancer condition. If she decides to proceed with gene testing, she says she wants the information for her daughters to have available in the future if they want it, although she adds that if she is found to have BRCA mutation, she would then consider prophylactic mastectomy and oophorectomy (removal of ovaries).

Objective Data

- Predicted probability for a BRCA1 mutation: Couch model: 18.7% (Fries et al. 2002).
- Predicted probability for a BRCA1 mutation: Shattuck Eidens model: 10.1%.
- Frank model noncontributory since no other relatives diagnosed with breast cancer under 50.
- > 10% likelihood for a familial BRCA1 mutation. (In most cancer risk assessment centers, nurses, genetic counselors, and related providers consult the American Society of Clinical Oncology statement published in 2003 for estimation of the presence of one or more mutations for specific forms of cancer. Prior to the publication of this statement, a 10% threshold was used to distinguish among patients and family members for whom a BRCA1/BRCA2 mutation was more or less likely. Currently, the clinical history and interpretation of the entire family picture by qualified providers of cancer risk assessment contribute to the estimation of the presence of a BRCA1/BRCA2 mutation. Mutation probability models are still used to quantify the risk, but the overall clinical picture and subsequent interpretation of the patient and family history prevail in discussions of risk.)

(Information about models used in cancer risk assessment may be accessed at the National Cancer Institute's web site: http://www.cancer.gov/cancerinfo/pdq/genetics/breast-and-ovarian/healthprofessional#section_79; additional references available on request).

Assessment: Knowledge Deficit

- The genetics of cancer.
- Breast cancer recurrence risk-reduction/early detection strategies.
- Risk assessment model interpreting genetic tests and breast cancer risk.
- Appropriate person to test for most meaningful genetic testing results.

- Determining appropriate candidate-families for genetic testing.
- Implications of genetic testing.
- Implications of a positive or negative genetic test.
- Implications of a gene test of uncertain significance.
- Options related to genetic testing outcomes.
- Decisional conflict: regarding whether to pursue genetic testing.
- We discussed the implications of the consultand having gene testing done when her daughters are this young and how she would handle telling or not telling them results. She said she needs to think about this more closely.
- Altered Family Process, potential for, regardless of what genetic testing decision is made.
- Familial Coping, potential for growth, if communication and information is well-handled.

Plan and Invervention

- Discuss and review the importance of monthly self–breast exam (consultand reports that she does do this); done early November.
- Discuss and review the importance of regular screening mammography once or twice per year (depending on physician recommendation); done early November.
- Discuss and review the importance of regular clinical breast exam by a qualified healthcare professional twice yearly; done early November.
- Discuss transvaginal ultrasound and CA-125 levels; done early November.
- Genetic counseling session (initial session completed in early November; entailed discussion of patient's expectations for genetic counseling and testing, basic explanation of mechanisms of inherited mutations for cancer, the process of risk estimation for the presence of selected mutations based on patient and family history, the implications of the results of genetic testing for the patient and her family, support resources for coping with the results of genetic testing, and resources for testing and protection of confidentiality of findings for the patient and her family).
- Informed consent for genetic testing (reviewed early November).
- Send summary letter for counseling session (sent early November).
- Provide consultand with commercial genetic testing laboratory customer assistance information to pursue insurance coverage for testing (given early November).
- Provide copy of "Understanding Gene Testing" (done early November; source available upon request).
- Provide copy of "Things to Think About Between Counseling Sessions" (done early November; source available upon request).
- Provide copy of Cancer Center gene testing consent form and informational packet to consultand (done early November; source available upon request).
- Follow-up and support by phone or in person as necessary.

Evaluation/Follow-Up (six months later)

The consultand and I had several telephone contacts since her genetic counseling session in November. She is having difficulty getting comfortable with a decision about whether to have genetic testing "either way." I asked if she wanted to come back in for further discussion. While she appreciated this offer, she feels that she understands the information, but until her counseling session she was unaware of all of the potential implications of testing, especially regarding her daughters and other family members. She feels that she is still "reeling" from the past two years and may need some more time to sort things out and feel comfortable with what exactly she would do with any genetic testing information if she were to proceed with this. I told her that this was fine (and not unusual to feel this way), but if she continued to have a dilemma regarding decision-making, I could also refer her to a psychologist who has a special interest in this area. She said that she would consider this option, but that for now she needed some more time to sort this out with her husband. I told her that I would always be available to her for more information, to give her the name and contact information of our psychologist, who has experience with cancer patients and issues unique to them, or just to talk. She told me she would probably recontact me sometime during the summer.

References

American Society of Clinical Oncology. (2003). Policy statement update: Genetic testing for carrier susceptibility. *Journal of Clinical Oncology, 21*, 2396–2406.

Fries, M. H., Holt, C., Carpenter, I., Carter, C. L., Daniels, J., Flanagan, J., Murphy, K., Hailey, B. J., Martin, L., Hume, R., Hudson, G., Cadman, M., Weatherly, R., & Nunes, M. E. (2002). Diagnostic criteria for testing for BRCA1 and BRCA2: The experience of the Department of Defense Familial Breast/Ovarian Cancer Research Project. *Military Medicine, 167*, 99–103.

Schneider, K. A. (1995). *Counseling about cancer: Strategies for genetic counselors.* Wallingford, PA: National Society of Genetic Counselors.

Prenatal Case Study
Dale Halsey Lea, MPH, RN, CGC, APNG, FAAN

Background

A local obstetrician called our genetics service to refer a prenatal patient with an abnormal amniocentesis result. The obstetrician told me that he had provided the pre-amniocentesis counseling for advanced maternal age and performed the amniocentesis in his office. The amniocentesis results showed that the baby was a female with an extra X chromosome (47,XXX). In this case, he was requesting an emergency genetic consultation for his patient, so that she could learn more about what the diagnosis meant for her baby, and decide how she would proceed in the pregnancy. The patient was referred to our service that day. At the time of consultation she was at 17 weeks gestation. Her husband was a transportation worker and was out of the area at the time of our initial visit.

In our genetics service, I am the primary provider of genetic counseling to prenatal patients in consultation with our medical geneticist.

Date of Visit

January

Nursing Interventions and Nursing Activities

Risk Identification—Genetic

History of Present Condition

Mrs. B. is a 37-year-old G2 P1 pregnant white female in apparently good health. She was 17 weeks and 4 days based on an expected date of confinement—delivery of her pregnancy (EDC) of the following June at the time of our meeting. Mrs. B. told us that her pregnancy was complicated by ongoing nausea for which she was being treated with Compazine suppositories. She was also taking thyroid supplementation because of her history of a papillary follicular carcinoma of the thyroid diagnosed in 1985.

Mrs. B. chose to have amniocentesis because of her maternal age of 37 years at delivery and the increased risk for chromosomal abnormalities. Amniocentesis was performed in the month prior to our visit. The results of amniocentesis revealed 47,XXX in all metaphase cells examined by the cytogenetics laboratory. Mrs. B. had many questions about the nature and cause of the chromosomal abnormality diagnosed in her baby. She sought more detailed information about 47,XXX and her options at this point.

Past Medical History

Mrs. B.'s past medical history was significant for papillary follicular carcinoma of the thyroid diagnosed in 1985. She underwent radioactive iodine treatment at that time, and has taken thyroid supplementation since. She reported that she has never smoked cigarettes and did not use alcohol. There were no other potentially teratogenic exposures (during pregnancy, a term used for an agent or factor that can affect genetic development and cause abnormalities of form or function or both [birth defects] in a fetus) during the pregnancy. She did not have any allergies. Her immunizations were up-to-date. Her medical history was otherwise noncontributory.

Current Medications

Thyroid supplementation, Compazine suppositories (to control nausea), daily prenatal vitamins that Mrs. B. was taking prior to getting pregnant to decrease the risk for open neural tube defect (result from a failure in closure of the spinal column in early pregnancy, for example, spina bifida or anencephaly) in her developing fetus.

Family History

A three-generation family history was obtained on both Mrs. B. and her husband (see pedigree below). In the review of family history, Mrs. B. informed us of the following issues of significance:

- Mrs. B. is one of seven siblings. She has an older brother who was diagnosed to have schizophrenia in his early 20s, and who has been hospitalized multiple times for this condition.
- A younger sister, age 36 years, has a history of mental illness (depression), with onset in her 20s, who also has been hospitalized and received treatment.
- Another sister has severe rheumatoid arthritis and her mother also has a history of arthritis.
- Mrs. B.'s maternal grandfather's sister's son is said to have had two sons who died from Duchenne Muscular Dystrophy (an X-linked inherited form of muscular dystrophy).
- Mr. B. has a history of learning disabilities.

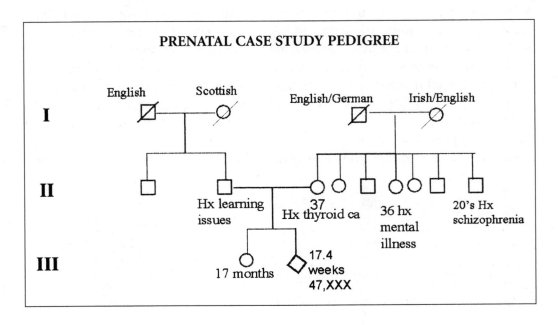

PRENATAL CASE STUDY PEDIGREE

Mrs. B.'s maternal grandparents are of English and Irish descent, and her paternal grandparents are of English and German descent. Mr. B.'s paternal grandparents are of English ancestry; his maternal grandparents are of Scottish descent. There is no consanguinity.

Objective

Mrs. B. was tearful during the initial phase of the interview. She expressed that she felt anxious and concerned about what the findings would mean. Since this was a prenatal genetic consultation and the focus was on explaining the abnormal chromosomal results and decision-making, a physical examination of Mrs. B. was not indicated.

Laboratory Results

Amniocentesis Chromosomal Analysis: 47,XXX—a copy of these results was faxed to us by the obstetrician prior to the consultation as verification of the prenatal diagnosis.

Social History

Mrs. B. told us that she has been married for five years. Both she and her husband completed college. Mrs. B. worked as a secretary for a small retail sales company prior to having children. Her husband was a construction worker and currently out of the area for a three-month period. His schedule was three months away and one month home. Mrs. B. said that she was trying to reach him with the news so that he could come home on emergency leave. Mr. and Mrs. B. have a 17-month old daughter at home who is in good health. She told us that this current pregnancy was planned.

Family Profile

Mr. and Mrs. B. live in a rural town about two hours north of our genetics clinic. They have a small house and a dog. Mrs. B.'s parents live in the same town nearby and provide support for Mrs. B. when her husband is away for three months at a time. Mr. B.'s family lives in the northern part of the state and visits during holidays. Mrs. B. said that they are a close family, too, and call her frequently when Mr. B. is away.

Medical Diagnosis and Plan

Prenatal Diagnosis: Chromosomal abnormality—47,XXX

Plan:

- Genetic counseling for Mrs. B. (assessment, communicating information about the disorder and risk, support for decisions, follow-up plans).
- Perinatal ultrasound examination at 18 weeks to rule out congenital anomalies (such as congenital heart defects, spina bifida, and genitourinary defects). Scheduled with perinatologist for January.

- Consider maternal chromosomal analysis to rule out the possibility of 47,XXX in Mrs. B.
- Follow-up genetic counseling when Mr. B. returns.

Genetic Assessment and Counseling with Mrs. B.

1) Issue/Theme: Mrs. B. had many questions about how her baby got the extra X chromosome. She asked whether it could have been caused by anything she or her husband might have been exposed to during the pregnancy and in the past.

Assessment: Lack of understanding and recognition of the association of advanced maternal age and increased risk for chromosomal abnormalities.

Nursing Diagnosis: Knowledge Deficit Disease Process

Nursing Outcome: Enhanced Knowledge

Nursing Interventions and Nursing Actions:
- Ensure privacy and confidentiality. I assured Mrs. B. that all information discussed and shared in the consultation and medical record information was maintained private and confidential unless Mrs. B. provided written consent. Mrs. B. asked that a summary letter be sent to her obstetrician.
- Provide information about natural history of disease. In response to Mrs. B.'s expressed concern about whether an exposure may have caused the chromosomal abnormality, I reassured Mrs. B. that nothing she or her husband did or were exposed to caused the chromosome problem in their baby. I provided written and visual information about chromosomes using graphics in Greenwood Genetics Genetic Counseling Booklet (Greenwood Genetic Center, 2002).
- I explained that the cause of 47,XXX is nondisjunction, or failure of the paired sex chromosomes to divide during meiosis in the gamete. This occurs prior to conception and there is no known cause or exposure(s) known to cause this to happen. Explained that extra or missing sex chromosomes (called sex chromosome aneuploidy) is common and is detected in about 1 in every 250 amniocenteses. The frequency of the diagnosis of 47,XXX by genetic amniocentesis is estimated to be 1 in 1000, the same as the incidence in the newborn population.

2) Issue/Theme: Mrs. B. had many questions about how the extra X chromosome would affect her baby's growth and development. She asked, "Will she have any birth defects or mental retardation?"

Assessment: Lack of knowledge about the impact of an extra X chromosome on physiological and mental development.

Nursing Diagnosis: Knowledge Deficit Growth and Development

Nursing Outcome: Enhanced Knowledge

Nursing Interventions and Nursing Actions:

- Provide information about natural history of disease, treatment, management, and prevention strategies. I reviewed the most current literature about 47,XXX. I explained to Mrs. B. that several studies have been carried out to look at the prospective growth and development of girls with 47,XXX. We reviewed these findings with Mrs. B., and provided her with literature regarding the prospective studies carried out to date. Specifically, I shared with her that 47,XXX infants are not generally distinguishable from children who have normal chromosomes in the first year of life, even though a slight delay in motor development has been observed in some affected children.

- Mrs. B. had questions about the nature and type of developmental delays. I explained to her that by two years of age, developmental delays in speech and language often become evident, and speech therapy is often necessitated in preschool years. Early school problems identified in some 47,XXX girls include speech and language deficiencies, lack of coordination, poor academic performance, and immature behavior; these persisted throughout school years for some of the girls. By high school age, girls with 47,XXX are generally tall. Sexual development is generally normal. Furthermore, I informed her that the only consistent physical characteristic in girls with 47,XXX is tall stature (above the 80th percentile) by adolescence. Sexual development and puberty are normal. Fertility is not reduced. I explained to Mrs. B. that, as with all individuals, variability among girls with 47,XXX is great. Some girls with the condition have attended college while others have had more difficulty in school. I shared with her that it has been observed that although mental retardation is unlikely, the IQ of girls with 47,XXX will probably be, on average, 10 to 15 points lower than that of their siblings. An approach of "anticipatory guidance" (alertness to the appearance of health problems that may occur with a condition over time; for example, regular developmental assessments to evaluate for developmental delays in the case of children with certain chromosome abnormalities) has been recommended as most helpful in identifying the onset of problems and providing appropriate interventions.

- Provide referral for community, local, and national resources, including support groups. I copied several studies and patient support information from the Genetic Alliance specific to the condition such as their web site, www.geneticalliance.org. I also provided information about the Triple X Support Group with their web site, www.triplo-x.org.

- I reviewed this information with her, sharing that in the most recent study by Robinson, Bender, and Linden (1991). Individuals with sex chromosome abnormalities diagnosed prenatally were progressing developmentally at a rate comparable to their siblings and were doing better at school and in peer relations than the group diagnosed *postnatally*. This is believed to be attributable to the supportive environment provided by their families, who made a conscious decision to continue their pregnancy. We talked about the possibility of physical anomalies in girls with 47,XXX. I shared with Mrs. B. that a few reports in the literature document physical anomalies diagnosed in females with 47,XXX, particularly renal, uterine, and vertebral anomalies providing evidence of the possible association between trisomy X and genitourinary defects.

▍ Monitor response when patient learns of implications for her baby. I asked Mrs. B. how she felt after hearing the above information about potential growth and developmental issues for girls with triple X. Mrs. B. said that she felt better having this information and that it "was not as bad as I had thought it would be." At the end of our genetic counseling session, Mrs. B. was able to convey that she understood the information about the condition, how it occurred, and the developmental and health implications for girls with 47,XXX. She made plans to have a follow-up ultrasound examination later in January, following our consultation. She took all of the printed information I shared with her home to review with her husband. She planned to return for follow-up counseling with her husband.

Plan:
We recommended that Mrs. B. have a high-resolution ultrasound examination for further evaluation for congenital anomalies. I coordinated the referral through her obstetrician. This was scheduled for later in January, following our consultation.

3) Issue/Theme: Mrs. B. asked what this prenatal diagnosis result meant in terms of future pregnancies. She stated: "My husband and I had been thinking of having other children. What does this mean in terms of our chances in future pregnancies to have a normal child?"

Assessment: Concern about the impact of prenatal diagnosis of an X chromosome on future reproduction and recurrence risks.

Nursing Diagnosis: Knowledge Deficit

Nursing Outcome: Enhanced Knowledge; Risk Detection and Health-Seeking Behavior

Nursing Interventions and Nursing Actions:
▍ Provide estimates of patient's risk based on phenotype, family history, or genotype. I reassured Mrs. B. that based on the literature reports of other couples who have had a pregnancy with 47,XXX, it was most likely that she and her husband would have a normal outcome in a future pregnancy. I reviewed with Mrs. B. that there are rare reports in the literature of infants with 47,XXX born to women who have 47,XXX. In this instance the chance of recurrence would be increased. I therefore recommended that Mrs. B.

consider having a chromosomal analysis to rule out this small possibility, and to gain further information about her chance of recurrence. I explained that the chance of recurrence for future pregnancies in females with normal chromosomes is likely to be slightly higher than the woman's age-related risk. Amniocentesis would be offered in any of Mrs. B.'s future pregnancies because of her maternal age and her history of having a pregnancy with 47,XXX.

Since we had reviewed the family history, I took the opportunity to convey to Mrs. B. that the family history of Duchenne Muscular Dystrophy was not expected to increase the risk for that condition in this or any future pregnancy. Mrs. B. said that she was not worried about this history, but was concerned about the family history of mental illness. We briefly talked about the potential hereditary disposition for mental illness in some families and the importance of early intervention. I also took the opportunity to reinforce the importance of taking daily folic acid for the prevention of birth defects.

▌ Monitor response when patient learns about genetic risks. Mrs. B. was able to explain the implications of the prenatal diagnosis for future reproduction. She said that she wanted to do "everything I can." She decided to go forward with having a chromosome analysis done for further evaluation.

Plan:
I offered to meet with Mrs. B. in follow-up to evaluate the other family history issues in greater depth if she desired. She said she wanted to discuss this with her husband first.

4) Issue/Theme: Mrs. B. explained that she really needed to talk with her husband about all she had learned about 47,XXX and the impact on their baby. She told me that she and her husband had talked about the possibility of a problem before the amniocentesis. She said that she just never thought it would happen. The couple had decided that they would only end a pregnancy if the condition was life-threatening in any way. She said that she did not think that they would decide to end the pregnancy based on what she knew now, but she needed time to let the information sink in.

Assessment: Difficulty choosing between alternatives.

Nursing Diagnosis: Decisional Conflict

Nursing Outcome: Participation: Healthcare Decisions

Nursing Interventions and Nursing Actions:
▌ Provide decision-making support. I reviewed with Mrs. B. her options at this point—to continue or to end her pregnancy. I explained that in such a situation, there are no right or wrong choices; each individual or couple makes the choice that is best for them based on personal beliefs and values.

I supported her decision to talk with her husband, and encouraged her to discuss the information with her obstetrician. I explored with her whether she had any other family members or friends she could talk with. Mrs. B. said she had one good friend that she could talk with. I also provided her with our 800 telephone number and my home phone number, and explained that it is our policy to remain available 24 hours a day to patients who are in a prenatal decision-making process. I encouraged her to call me with any questions.

▪ Provide a written summary of the genetic counseling process to the client and referral source. I informed Mrs. B. that I would summarize our consultation in a letter to her obstetrician and would send a copy to her as well. I encouraged her to call with any questions she or her husband might have.

Plan:

Mrs. B. made plans to return for follow-up genetic counseling when her husband returned so that he could come and hear the same information and share in the decision with her. We planned to meet again later in January for further discussion of the prognosis and their options.

Genetic Assessment and Counseling with Mrs. B. in Follow-Up with Her Husband

1) Issue/Theme: When Mrs. B. and her husband arrived for follow-up, they told me that they had read all of the information we had provided about 47,XXX. Mrs. B. had the high-resolution ultrasound examination, and Mr. B. was able to be present for this. They told me that the ultrasound was completely normal and did not show any of the birth defects that have been associated with 47,XXX. They expressed relief about this result and told me that this had a big impact on their decision.

Assessment: Decision-making and choosing between alternatives.

Nursing Diagnosis: Decision-Making

Nursing Diagnosis: Participation: Healthcare Decisions

Nursing Interventions and Nursing Actions:
▪ Provide decision-making support. I reviewed with the couple the chromosomal basis of 47,XXX and the studies and literature about the condition. We talked at length about the potential for learning disabilities. Mr. B. offered that he had a history of learning disabilities when he was younger and got help in school, so this was not a significant issue for him. Mrs. B. agreed. The couple told me that they planned to continue the pregnancy and felt relieved and comfortable about their decision. I offered support of their decision to continue the pregnancy.

▪ Monitor response when patient learns of genetic risks. The couple expressed that the information I had provided had helped them to review their options and come to a decision that was comfortable for both of them. The normal results from the ultrasound further supported their decision to continue the pregnancy. They planned to continue to be followed by the obstetrician and deliver their baby in the medical center hospital nearby.

2) Issue/Theme: Mr. and Mrs. B. asked whether their baby should be followed by a specialist and whether there was anything special that needed to be done after birth.

Assessment: Need for plan for follow-up care.

Nursing Diagnosis: Knowledge Deficit Health Resources

Nursing Outcomes: Enhanced Knowledge

Nursing Interventions and Nursing Actions:

▌ Provide referral community resources. I recommended that Mr. and Mrs. B. make their pediatrician aware of the prenatal diagnosis of 47,XXX. I offered that we would be glad to see their baby in the newborn period for evaluation if they desired. Furthermore, I recommended that their baby have a chromosomal analysis for confirmation of the prenatal diagnosis. Mr. and Mrs. B. agreed to these suggestions, and asked me to send a copy of the counseling summary to their pediatrician.

▌ Monitor response when patient learns of genetic risks. After their baby was born, Mr. and Mrs. B. wrote a letter to me expressing their gratitude for the genetic counseling and how the process had helped them. They offered to serve as resource to other couples in a similar situation. They expressed their thoughts and impressions about their experience in a satisfaction questionnaire response from our center.

Follow-Up Nursing Outcome Evaluation: Health-Seeking Behaviors and Hope
As a result of our offer to evaluate and follow their baby, Mrs. B. brought her daughter to our clinic for a genetic evaluation at three months of age. Her daughter was developing normally at the time. Mrs. B. told us that she had pursued our recommendation for further testing, and a chromosomal analysis had been done. This confirmed the diagnosis of 47,XXX. She also told us that she had had her own chromosomes checked and "they were normal too." She said that she and her husband were enjoying their daughter, and felt comfortable with the diagnosis and how they were managing as a family. They planned to have their daughter evaluated by genetics on an annual basis.

References

Greenwood Genetic Center. (2002) *Genetic Counseling Aids.* 4th ed. Greenville, SC: Keys Printing. Available online at www.ggc.org.

Robinson, A., Bender, B. G., & Linden, M. G. (1991). Summary of clinical findings in children and young adults with sex chromosome anomalies. *Birth Defects, 26,* 225–228.

Neurogenetics Case Study
Catherine Bove, MEd, RN, APNG

Background

MM is a 20-year-old female full-time college student who came to the Neurogenetics Clinic from Latin America. Her family is originally from Asia. MM is attending college as an economics major. She is the youngest of four; her two brothers are 33 and 32, and her sister is 30. None has any known health problems. Both her mother (age 63) and father (age 68) have hypertension. MM was diagnosed with neurofibromatosis (NF), type 1, when she was 13 years because of multiple café au lait spots, axillary freckling, and multiple typical small cutaneous neurofibromas on her trunk, back, arms, legs, and on her face. She had no ocular manifestations, no observable plexiform tumors noted on physical assessment, and no history of migraines or learning disabilities. These findings are often associated with NF, type 1. When she was diagnosed her family was examined and was told that no one else had NF and the appearance of this condition in her was a "new mutation." She stated that her parents were told she was healthy and most people with NF don't have major problems.

As far as MM was concerned, NF was a "skin disease" and the only discomfort she said she experienced was "social." She said she felt "embarrassed" when she was asked about her "brown spots" and the skin tumors. She said she never felt like NF could "make me sick." Her primary care provider while living in Boston is a nurse practitioner (NP) at her college. She feels confident in the care the NP provides because she "examines me carefully" and "takes time to listen to me."

On a weekend in the fall, MM was admitted to a local emergency room (ER) for assessment and treatment of acute, sudden chest pain. A computerized axial tomography (CAT) scan was done and a chest tumor was found, leading to a referral to a thoracic surgeon (a CAT scan is an x-ray that produces three-dimensional, computerized images of internal organs). After two weeks of testing it was determined that MM had a malignant change in a plexiform neurofibroma, and surgery was recommended. MM was encouraged to contact her family immediately. Her parents do not speak English or Spanish, and her siblings are more fluent in Spanish. MM speaks the language of her parents as well as Spanish and English. She says she is comfortable in all three languages because she studied all three since childhood. Her family owns a business in Latin America, and all her family lives and works there. The family made arrangements to come to Boston. MM's father stayed home to run the business but sent his wife and two of the older siblings. After the surgery and for the duration of the radiation treatment, her mother and sister rented an apartment near the hospital and took care of her. Several family meetings were held at the hospital, before, during, and after the surgery. Hospital interpreters were present for all meetings. MM's older siblings seemed to understand the gravity of the situation, but it was difficult to assess her mother's understanding. The mother seemed to know the chest tumor was malignant but acted as if there was no question that the doctors

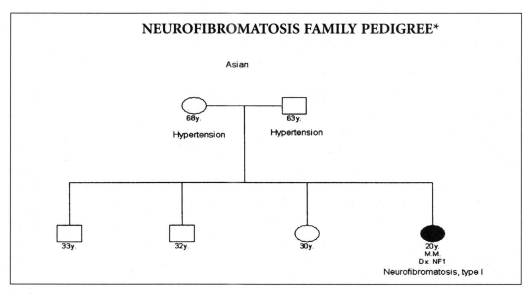

NEUROFIBROMATOSIS FAMILY PEDIGREE*

Asian

68y.
Hypertension

63y.
Hypertension

33y.

32y.

30y.

20y.
M.M.
Dx: NF1
Neurofibromatosis, type I

*This family pedigree does not show three generations because those data are unavailable.

could "cure" her daughter. MM and her siblings did not let the interpreter contradict the mother when she made statements that indicated a cure was expected. I attempted several times to refer MM's mother to a hospital social worker who could speak their languages, but they refused; her sister said, "We can take care of our mother's needs, a social worker for support isn't necessary."

History of Present Illness

In the summer prior to this episode, MM had an annual NF examination in Latin America. A cranial magnetic resonance imaging (MRI) scan was done and showed a single T2 bright lesion in the left parietal occipital area, consistent with a typical unidentified bright objects (UBOs) have been observed on cranial imaging (MRI) in many children with NF, type 1, and the clinical significance of these findings is still under study. There were no brain tumors. She also had a chest MRI that showed a large apical tumor, and a pelvic MRI scan showed multiple deep nodules and sacral roots, extending out into the pelvis. All of these tumors had all been previously evaluated over the past several years, and no changes were noted. MM states she felt well, had no pain, and did not feel these tumors caused any health problems.

In the fall (as noted above), she experienced acute onset severe mid-back pain. The pain lasted throughout the day and worsened on lying down. She had no recent trauma or change in physical activity. The pain proceeded to radiate to her anterior chest. She went to the ER of the local hospital. A chest x-ray was abnormal and a CAT scan was obtained, which showed a 6 × 4.5-cm mass in the right apex. She was referred to a thoracic surgeon for a biopsy. The nurse practioner who followed MM referred her to the Genetics Clinic because she wanted MM's overall management to be comprehensive and felt the decision for surgery should be made by a team of professionals experienced with NF, type 1. The chest scan demonstrated a lesion that was most likely a plexiform neurofibroma. The neurologist, after a careful neurological exam, ordered a positron emission tomography (PET) scan to ascertain if the mass was malignant (a PET scan measures changes in blood flow associated with brain function by detecting positrons, radioactively labeled substances that have been injected into the body).

In the experience of our clinic, sudden-onset, intractable pain can be a cardinal symptom of a malignant degeneration of a plexiform tumor. The concern for patients with NF, type 1, who have a plexifrom tumor is that they have a lifetime risk of 5% to 10% for a malignant degeneration is of this type of tumor. Our experience has shown that the risk for degeneration, on average, peaks around the third and fourth decade of life.

Medical Diagnosis

MM, because of her diagnosis of NF, type 1, was referred to the Genetics Clinic for evaluation of complaints of severe right scapular chest. She is a well-developed, well-nourished female in no acute distress.

Head: Low set.

Ears, Nose, and Throat: Normocephalic, atraumatic.

Eyes: Normal, pupils equal, round, reactive to light, accommodation, moist mucous membranes, and extraocular movements were intact.

Neck: No jugular venous distention, no bruits.

Neuro: Examination essentially normal, her gait and station were normal, as was her cranial nerve examination. Her reflexes were 2–3+ and symmetrical. Motor strength, tone, and bulk were normal.

Although MM's pain had lessened since the ER admission and was not severe, she did still complain of intermittent pain. She denied shortness of breath, cough, hemoptysis, headache, visual disturbances, angina, melena, and abdominal pain. She had lost about eight pounds over the month prior to the pain onset, and she reported fatigue.

The patient has had no previous surgery. The patient denied diabetes mellitus, myocardial infarction, coronary artery disease, tuberculosis, and liver and thyroid disease. No known drug allergies. The MRI scan showed a 7-cm apical mass along the right superior mediastinum with invasion into the mediastinum and right apical chest wall. Numerous enlarged tubular structures bilaterally were noted to follow the course of the nerve roots. This area lit up on PET scan intensely. A needle biopsy showed an atypical nerve sheath tumor suspicious for low-grade malignancy.

She was referred for surgical resection and underwent a complete resection of the right apical superior sulcus tumor in the fall during the following weeks. The surgery went well and her physical recovery was uneventful. The tumor was completely removed but the margins towards the chest wall were minimal. A course of treatment by radiotherapy (RT) was recommended in order to reduce the risk of local recurrence. The final pathology report affirmed the diagnosis of a grade 2/3 sarcoma. A course of six weeks of radiation was undertaken for five days a week.

Nursing Diagnosis

Knowledge Deficit: Signs/symptoms of NF, type 1

Risk for malignancy
Pain
Fatigue secondary to radiotherapy
Risk for social isolation
Altered parent/adult-offspring relationship
Genetic counseling
Powerlessness
Spiritual distress (distress of the human spirit)
Anxiety
Depression
Sleep pattern disturbance
Body image disturbance
Personal identity disturbance

Nursing Interventions

My first meeting with MM was during her second visit to the Genetics Clinic in the fall. I asked about her pain and she said it had recently subsided and it wasn't the same intensity as it was a few weeks before. Initially MM denied being anxious about the impending surgery and the possibility of a malignancy. Her defensive coping made it difficult to assess how much she actually understood about the potentially serious consequences of the chest tumor. MM appeared to be somewhat socially and emotionally immature. Her behavior was more like that of a young adolescent. I asked her if she would like to utilize our first visit by discussing what NF, type 1, has meant to her both socially and in terms of health issues. She replied she had not directly asked her doctors at home (in her native country) any questions about NF. She said the doctors always addressed her mother as if she were only a child even though she was an adolescent. I asked her what she did know about NF, type 1, and the health problems associated with this disorder. She said her mother took her to a genetic clinic at home for the diagnosis and for annual follow-up. She thinks her mother was told NF usually "wasn't anything to worry about" but she didn't actually remember being told anything else except "NF is café au lait spots and small skin tumors."

I encouraged her to tell me about the emotional impact NF had on her life prior to learning about her chest tumor. MM seemed eager to talk and seemed appreciative for the opportunity to discuss her questions, concerns, and emotional reactions. It was apparent that MM wanted to learn more about NF and that she wanted to talk about her feelings. It appeared that the concept of a malignant tumor was so overwhelmingly powerful that MM couldn't yet focus on it. It seemed a necessity for her to first learn and understand "her NF" before she could handle the magnitude of conceptualizing a malignancy. Over time, I had several counseling sessions with her.

The nurse practitioner caring for MM had referred her to the psychologist at the college's counseling department, and I spoke with her therapist a number of times. The therapist felt it was valuable for MM to discuss the NF issues with me because of my experience with the health and psychosocial concerns that people affected by NF encountered. The therapist thought we could both offer support and counseling during this crisis and then she could treat MM on a long-term basis over her next two years of college.

During the meetings I had with MM, we focused on her experiences related to her NF diagnosis, and in this context she described her emotional state. She has been struggling with the social issues that many adolescents verbalize regarding the cutaneous manifestations of the skin tumors and "brown spots." She expressed feelings of distress when "people look at my lumps and spots." I also inquired about her understanding of the genetic issues and asked if she ever had genetic counseling. She responded immediately that she not been counseled about the genetic information. She recently was attracted to a student in her dormitory. This attraction made her want to learn about her "genetic risks." MM said she hadn't dated much and didn't actually have a relationship with the young man she was attracted, to but this experience made her think about genetics. She said, "It's going to be something I'll have to face someday." We reviewed the inheritance, and her questions indicated she understood the concept of dominant inheritance (the trait is usually manifested in the person with the genetic mutation, and there is a 50% risk of passing the mutation to offspring). She said genetics would be a "big decision" when she was thinking about marriage.

She was followed in the NF clinic on a monthly basis, and we continued our discussions at every visit. During this period she underwent the chest surgery and postoperatively was treated with radiation. We noted that midway through the radiation therapy, she became clinically depressed. I spoke with a social worker in Oncology about treatment for the depression with medication (recommended). After much discussion, MM agreed she was willing to be treated with antidepressant medication. She said the medication helped her to be able to "mentally focus" so she could continue to study for her college courses and "get my life back." She felt she needed to remain in school and focus on her studies in order to cope with the radiation. Her plan was to come off the medication when she completes her radiotherapy.

Later, after MM completed the RT, she began to ask direct questions about what the requirements will be for long-term and careful management of her plexiform tumor. She also discussed the risk for recurrence of these tumors. Although the tumor was completely removed, its margins along the chest wall were minimal. The concern that the surgical team had was that tumor can seed through the chest wall. Very careful monitoring would be necessary for at least the next decade. MM was just beginning to comprehend the possibility that a malignancy could reoccur. We are presently talking about the grieving process because she feels a "sense of loss about myself" (in terms of her shortened life expectancy), and these grieving feelings reflect her emotional experiences since her surgery for the malignancy.

In our most recent discussion she told me she had been struggling with her "sense of identity" long before the NF tumor became the focus. She told me she didn't know what she wanted from her life. She felt she was studying business because it was what her family expected. "My family expects me to work with them in their hotel business." But over time, she said she had been thinking of studying to become a teacher of students who are blind. "I know being blind isn't part of NF 1, so I'm not influenced by that. I want to help blind kids learn. I'm looking into schools where I can major in teaching children with disabilities." At this point, I allowed MM to express her feelings and provided emotional support.

Health Teaching

Knowledge of disorder, its management, and treatment.

Psychosocial Adjustment: Personal identity disturbance—therapeutic listening and supportive coping enhancement, including inspiring hop.

Case management/coordination of care: NF, type 1, requires both coordination and continuity of care as well as ongoing collaboration with other healthcare professionals in order to provide comprehensive patient care. Because the condition has multiple manifestations, and psychological adaptations can be challenging across the lifespan, an interdisciplinary team approach (including social worker, RN, and neurologist) is valuable with patients and families with or at risk for this condition. In addition, the healthcare team must be sensitive to the cultural values and expectations held by patients and family members (for example, in this situation MM was expected to finish her studies and work in the family business) who may have questions and/or be at risk for heritable conditions such as NF, type 1.

Planning

This young woman's plan of care must be patient-centered and sensitive to her cultural beliefs and values. It must reflect her gradual adjustment to her acknowledgment of the serious consequences of a possibly malignant tumor. The plan of care uses outcome indicators based on the natural history of this disorder. Ongoing psychosocial support will also be important. The patient's evaluation of her management needs to be solicited after her frequent examination. Her family also needs to be included in the planning on an ongoing basis because the patient receives care and support from her family.

Outcome Identification: The ongoing collection of comprehensive patient information is crucial for management of symptoms and to decide what treatment modalities will be future options.

1. Outcome knowledge: disease process and treatment regimen
2. Acceptance: health status
3. Knowledge of genetics
4. Grief resolution
5. Social support
6. Care reflects current clinical management standards
7. Plan of care involves patient and her family developed in collaboration with family and professionals

Evaluation Statement

I have been following MM over these past six months and have observed the many changes in her personal development during this stressful time. I see that my relationship with her will be ongoing and supportive. Her prognosis is guarded because sarcomas in NF, type 1, are difficult to treat. Many of these tumors don't respond to treatment and can recur over the next decade or sooner. The quality of MM's life will require that she make decisions that are based on accurate knowledge that has been presented to her, with sensitivity to her personal and cultural values and beliefs. I felt that a climate of acceptance, therapeutic listening, and offering MM feedback during our discussions could identify and clarify her views and beliefs—in other words, telling her the truth about her healthcare status while recognizing that she and her family may interpret that information according to their own belief systems. Supportive counseling and health information will be offered in the context of her opinions and emotional responses. Supporting MM will require a delicate balance between presenting reality and preserving hope.

Discussion

These three case studies illustrate many of the performance indicators and characteristic components expected in case study texts (see discussions in Chapters 5–7) that are associated with the *Statement on the Scope and Standards of Genetics Clinical Nursing Practice* (International Society of Nurses in Genetics [ISONG] & American Nurses Association [ANA] 1998). These three cases provide the reader with a sample of the kinds of patients and families who seek genetic evaluation and counseling. The woman with familial cancer and her family constitute an example of the many thousands in the United States and across the world who are discovering that they have inherited a mutation for breast and ovarian cancer and fear for the future health of their children and grandchildren. The family expecting a child with a chromosomal abnormality discovered by prenatal diagnosis symbolizes the position of additional thousands of couples in childbearing years who request testing and hope for healthy newborns. The young college student who had been living with a diagnosis of neurofibromatosis, type 1, receives specialized diagnostic testing and genetic counseling for this condition, appearing as a new mutation in her and placing her offspring at

50% risk for inheriting this gene. The nurse, in each case, is applying the nursing process of assessment, diagnosis, planning, intervention, and evaluation with the patient and family. In addition, the nurse's narrative reflects sensitivity to the possible implications of testing for these genetic conditions and the results, positive or negative, for the patient, the families, and even the community.

A cardinal feature of the nurse's care includes a family pedigree, the diagram depicting the family health history, which is essential to understanding the inheritance patterns of illness in a kindred. The interpretation of the inheritance patterns are part of the responsibility of the Advanced Practice Nurse in Genetics, and the core components of genetic counseling include the description of the condition(s), their cause(s) as currently understood, and the prediction of (or absence of) risk of the condition(s) in other family members, including offspring. In these cases, the nurse acts as a coordinator of care aiming for seamless communication among the patient and family, the referring provider, and community resources.

The case studies, in concert with the other portfolio evidence, provide a very clear demonstration of the nurse's competence. The narratives of encounters with patients and families should reflect clinically appropriate care (accuracy of information, usability of resources, and evaluation of outcomes). The GNCC Score Team compares the content of the case studies along with the other portfolio contents and rates the quality of the evidence in each of the required areas (below standard, at standard, or above standard). The decisions of the members of the Score Team, taken as a whole, determine whether the credential is awarded to the applicant. Those applicants who receive the credential may then use it to affirm their qualifications to provide genetics nursing care.

In the case of genetics nursing, the clinician must continually be aware of the probabilities that testing for a genetic condition or susceptibility for a genetic condition generates responses throughout a family that are heavily influenced by cultural values and spiritual beliefs. Moreover, the presence of a genetic condition or susceptibility to a genetic condition affects family life decisions such as marriage and childbearing. Indeed, career choices and economic considerations (healthcare insurance, for example) may rest on the outcomes of gene-based testing. The gene-based diagnostic and therapeutic procedures handled by nurses in genetics differ profoundly from such testing as a complete blood count (CBC) or chest x-ray, which have implications for the individual's health but are less likely to affect family relationships.

As mentioned above, gene-based testing has implications for the community. Genetic screening for conditions detected at birth, such as phenylketonuria, hypothyroidism, and certain metabolic conditions (for example, the organic acidemias), is part of the newborn screening program in most parts of the Unites States. Social policies that provide support for screening, testing, and treatment of genetic conditions, including carrier screening for such conditions as sickle cell anemia and cystic fibrosis, are part of the framework of federal, state, and local public health programs. Moreover, testing for susceptibility to genetic conditions such as cancer have engendered heated debates about discrimination by insurance carriers—in some instances resulting in cancellation or denial of health coverage for those who test positive. The Office of Biotechnology Activities at the National Institutes of Health has a valuable web site that provides information and resources about these debates, the proceedings of the Advisory Committee on Genetics, Health, and Society of the U.S. Department of Health and Human Services (www4.od.nih.gov/oba).

In summary, these three cases illustrate the challenges in genetics nursing practice. They show the efforts of the nurses not only to serve the patient with regard to the diagnosis at hand, but also to address additional concerns for the long-term outcomes of nursing care and the future decision-making that may be necessary in the lives of the patient and his or her family. While each case reflects the authors' experiences and their individual practices, they also show the strengths of nurses who strive to practice according to ISONG and ANA's *Statement on the Scope and Standards of Genetics Clinical Nursing Practice* and who have been credentialed by the GNCC through the portfolio process.

Reference

International Society of Nurses in Genetics (ISONG) & American Nurses Association (ANA). (1998). *Statement on the scope and standards of genetics clinical nursing practice.* Washington, DC: ANA.

Appendix A
Glossary of Acronyms and Terms

ACCME Accreditation Council on Continuing Medical Education

ADA American Dietetic Association

ANA American Nurses Association

ANCC American Nurses Credentialing Center

AOTA American Occupational Therapy Association

APNG Advanced Practice Nurse in Genetics

CAP Clinical achievement portfolio

CAT Computerized axial tomography

CBC Complete blood count

CDR Commission on Dietetic Registration

CE Continuing education

CERP Continuing education recognition point

CEU Continuing education unit

CNO College of Nurses of Ontario

CNS Clinical Nurse Specialist

COC Commission on Certification (of the ANCC)

CPE Continuing professional education

CSL Center for Self-Sustaining Leadership

CV Curriculum vitae

ER Emergency room

FEN Faculty of Emergency Nursing (of the Royal College of Nursing)

GCN Genetics Clinical Nurse

GNCC Genetic Nursing Credentialing Commission

HIPAA Health Insurance Portability and Accountability Act

ISONG International Society of Nurses in Genetics

KSAs Knowledge, skills, and abilities (often observable and measurable in clinical nursing practice)

MRI Magnetic resonance imaging

NACNS National Association of Clinical Nurse Specialists

NBC National Board Certification

NBPTS National Board for Professional Teaching Standards

NCLEX National Council Licensure Examination

NCSBN National Council of State Boards of Nursing

NF Neurofibromatosis

NMC Nursing and Midwifery Council (United Kingdom)

NP Nurse practitioner

PDP Professional Development Portfolio

PDT Professional Development Tool

PET positron emission tomography

Portfolio A goal-oriented collection of evidence of competence (reports, logs, case studies, performance ratings, accomplishments, works in progress, and goals and plans for future activities; may include inventories and listings of possessions or properties); portfolio evidence is demonstrable and verifiable, most often in the form of documents, media, and related materials

Portfolio process Procedures whereby portfolios can be transmitted, received, evaluated, and their evidence quantified

PPP Professional Practice Profile (Oklahoma State Board of Nursing) or Personal Professional Profile (United Kingdom Central Council for Nurses, Midwives, and Health Visitors)

PREP Postregistration education and practice

RCN Royal College of Nursing

RT Radiotherapy

Score team Group of reviewers or evaluators who judge the quality of the portfolio contents

SME subject matter expert (a person knowledgeable about an area of specialization, such as specialized nursing practice)

SOAPIE Basic elements of standard documentation in the health professions: subjective data, objective data, assessment, plan, intervention, and evaluation

UBO unidentified bright object

UKCC United Kingdom Central Council for Nurses, Midwives, and Health Visitors

Appendix B
Selected Components of the GNCC Application Guidelines Packet with Sample Portfolio

One part of the *Portfolio Evaluation and Scoring Training Manual* is the GNCC Application Guidelines Packet. Several components of this extensive packet, which provides the basis upon which an applicant has created a portfolio, are reproduced in this appendix. (Selections of the manual itself are reproduced in Appendix C.)

The application packets for the APNG and GCN credentials include specific instructions regarding credentialing requirements, portfolio components, forms to be used, and examples, so that the expectations of the applicant and the evaluation criteria are clearly identified.

Information on how to obtain an official application packet can be found at the GNCC web site, www.geneticnurse.org. It is advisable to obtain the packet at least three months prior to portfolio submission since the packet contains instructions on how to assemble your portfolio, what you will need to include in your portfolio, forms you will need to use, and selected examples to assist you.

Chapters 4 and 6 contain more details about both this packet and the training manual.

**GENETIC NURSING
CREDENTIALING COMMISSION**

APPLICATION GUIDELINES PACKET
FOR
THE ADVANCED PRACTICE NURSE IN
GENETICS CREDENTIAL (APNG)
AND
THE GENETICS CLINICAL NURSE CREDENTIAL
(GCN)
2005 Credentialing Cycle Edition

GNCC logo by Jason Greco (DNA picture courtesy of DOE Human Genome Program http://www.ornl.gov/hgmis)

A FEW WORDS TO THE APPLICANT for the APNG or the GCN

Read ALL pages of this Application Packet and follow the directions provided. Information in the Call for Portfolios and in the Glossary will be valuable to the applicants. If you firmly believe that you qualify for the APNG or the GCN, but some aspect of your submission does not meet the stated requirement, please write a letter of explanation and the evidence meriting consideration of your application. This letter and evidence should be placed in the section of the portfolio to which it corresponds. Your letter and evidence will be examined by the appropriate GNCC, INC. Score Team according to the policies governing each credential award.

APPLICANTS MAY SUBMIT THEIR PORTFOLIOS FOR EITHER THE APNG OR THE GCN, NOT BOTH. Unsuccessful applicants for the APNG will not be awarded the GCN. Each credential stands alone as a separate entity. There is no limit to the number of times an individual may apply for the APNG or the GCN. The nurse retains the APNG or the GCN award for five years from issuance as long as he/she retains valid, unencumbered nurse licensure in the jurisdiction(s) of clinical practice. The APNG or the GCN award is renewable five years after it is issued.

The portfolio contents will be scored by a Score Team trained for this purpose. Scores are assigned in a range from well below expectations for the role (needs improvement) to well above expectations for the role. Portfolios with passing scores will have the majority of contents at the "meets or exceeds expectations" level. Applications will be designated as "passed" or "failed." Applicants who have received a "failed" designation may request a report outlining the strong and weak areas of their portfolio. Applicants have the right to appeal the "fail" designation until 31 December of the year in which the portfolio in question was submitted.

ALL PORTFOLIO SUBMISSIONS BECOME THE PROPERTY OF THE GNCC, INC. AND WILL NOT BE RETURNED TO THE APPLICANT. **THE ORIGINAL AND FOUR COPIES MUST BE SUBMITTED.**

Application Portfolios are due no later than 1 March 2005 and must be sent to:
Rita Black Monsen, DSN, MPH, RN
Executive Director, Genetic Nursing Credentialing Commission
119 Ledgerwood Circle
Hot Springs, AR 71913
Applicants will be notified of the results of the portfolio evaluation on or before 1 December.

Title and Rights of the APNG and the GCN
The Master's prepared nurse with the APNG credential will use these letters after his/her name, degree(s), and license(s). The Baccalaureate prepared nurse with the GCN will use these letters after his/her name, degree(s), and license(s). The APNG credential or the GCN credential will allow the nurse to receive recognition for his/her clinical practice abilities in appropriate health care settings. The APNG may provide the bases for advanced practice nurse licensure by state boards of nursing (or their equivalent) or reimbursement by third party payors (or their equivalent) depending upon the laws, regulations, and/or policies of the individual jurisdiction(s) where the nurse practices.

Fairness of evaluation, validity and reliability of ratings
The GNCC, INC. and ISONG have taken steps to assure fairness of evaluation (ratings) for all submissions and have contracted with a consultant firm, Center for Sustained Leadership, LLC. (CSL), to assure the validity and reliability of the portfolio requirements, the rating assignments, and the scoring procedures. We have designed the features of the portfolio process via widely accepted and sound practices associated with evaluation of professional performance.

Grounds for denial of the APNG award or the GCN award include, but are not limited to:
Receipt of portfolio after deadline
Incomplete portfolio (missing elements)
Breach of confidentiality and privacy of patient/family/client information
Inability of the GNCC, INC. Score Team to validate portfolio elements via random check of submitted materials

SECTION A

THE
ADVANCED PRACTICE NURSE IN GENETICS
CREDENTIAL
(APNG)

APPLICATION GUIDELINES

ONE ORIGINAL AND FOUR COPIES OF THE PORTFOLIO CONTENTS WILL BE SUBMITTED. APPLICANTS WILL NOT MAKE COPIES OF CONTENT IN SEALED ENVELOPES, BUT INCLUDE THESE IN THE PACKET OF ORIGINAL DOCUMENTS

PORTFOLIO COMPONENT See standard forms/recommendations for requirements *PORTFOLIO MUST CONTAIN ALL COMPONENTS LISTED*	INDICATORS FOR THE APNG		SCORING Scores will be given to components in the portfolio; final score will be calculated for over-all portfolio
	TYPES OF DOCUMENTS* See standard forms/recommendations for requirements VERIFIABLE EVIDENCE REQUIRED	COMMENTS Evidence will be randomly selected and verified by the appropriate GNCC, INC. Score Team	
Experience, Employment, Professional & Community Activities	**Curriculum Vitae(CV)** Each employment position should provide brief list of major responsibilities (and percent of time devoted to clinical care; education/teaching, administration, research, and/or other activities); CV should reflect 3 years of active membership in a related professional association; with active participation in at least one professional association committee **Log of 50 cases** Minimum of 50 cases which reflect applicant's nursing practice; cases must have received care within 5 years of application **4 Case Studies (MUST BE FROM CASE LOGS)** Subjective, Objective, Assessment, Plan (SOAPIE) format Identification of Patient, Family, and/or Community disguised by ID number or other code Date(s) of care; narrative account of history, assessment, minimum of three generation pedigree, nursing activities; counseling letters, educational materials prepared for clients Components reflecting one or more ISONG STANDARDS found in International Society of Nurses in Genetics, Inc. & American Nurses Association. (1998). <u>Statement on the scope and standards of genetics clinical nursing practice</u>. Washington, DC: American Nurses Publishing. Outcomes of nursing care **Letter of verification from Supervisor/Professional Colleague**; verifies that applicant has provided care to clients named in Log and/or Case Studies—must be sealed in envelope with signature on flap **Professional Performance Verification & Evaluation** form —must be sealed in envelope with signature on flap **Three Peer Reviews** see Professional Performance Verification & Evaluation form —must be sealed in envelope with signature on flap	Curriculum vitae (CV) Experience as a clinical genetics nurse with >50% genetic practice component (includes completion of at least 300 hours of genetic practicum [clinical] experiences). Log of 50 cases-40 OF THE 50 CASES MUST BE POST-GRADUATION FROM MASTERS PROGRAM 4 Case Studies-ALL MUST BE POST-GRADUATION FROM MASTERS PROGRAM Licenses(s) Certificate(s) Log and Case Studies must reflect the ISONG Scope and Standards of Practice, a knowledge base of basic genetic principles; inheritance patterns, risk for genetic conditions in patients and families, construction and interpretation of pedigrees; interpretation of laboratory findings and diagnostic test results provision of genetic counseling, and follow-up. Letter of verification must be on organization or agency letterhead **OF THE THREE KINDS OF DOCUMENTS (Letter of Verification, Performance Appraisal, and Peer Review) AT LEAST ONE MUST BE FROM A GENETIC HEALTH PROFESSIONAL,** i.e. MD/PhD geneticist, CGC, APNG, or doctorally prepared nurse with training in genetics	ISONG STANDARDS OF CARE AND PERFORMANCE INDICATORS will be used in the over-all process of evaluating the portfolio contents

PORTFOLIO COMPONENT See standard forms/recommendations for requirements *PORTFOLIO MUST CONTAIN ALL COMPONENTS LISTED*	INDICATORS FOR THE APNG		SCORING
	TYPES OF DOCUMENTS* See attached standard forms/recommendations for requirements ***VERIFIABLE EVIDENCE REQUIRED***	**COMMENTS** Evidence will be randomly selected and verified by the appropriate GNCC, INC. Score Team	Scores will be given to components in the portfolio; final score will be calculated for over-all portfolio
Formal and Informal Education REQUIRED COURSE CONTENT (Genetic topics) Human Genetics Molecular and Biochemical Genetics Ethical, Legal, and Social Issues Clinical Applications of Genetics including Genetic Counseling, Genetic Variations in Populations	**RN license** and, if applicable, certifications(s) (copies) Transcripts (originals in sealed envelopes required) Completed Baccalaureate in Nursing and Masters in Nursing (completed Masters in related field accepted for the last time in 2005 cycle) Credit courses or Continuing education in Genetics <ul><li>Didactic (lectures)</li><li>Laboratory</li><li>Clinical practice component</li></ul> Education must show attendance at offerings within five years of the application Self-study (evidence must be verifiable) Certification by American Board of Medical Genetics and/or American Board of Genetic Counseling very significant as evidence Other (as submitted by applicant)	Curriculum vitae (able to cross-check attendance at education programming) Transcripts (original; required even if no genetics content is shown) Certificates of course attendance and/or contact hours in continuing education—minimum of 50 contact hours in the past 5 years; letters confirming attendance if transcripts and/or certificates not available. Content in genetic topics must be in evidence	
Teaching, Educational Efforts **Other achievements**	Educational programs Presentations and/or lectures at professional conferences Presentations and/or lectures at worksite conferences Courses (in accredited schools and continuing education) Presentations and/or lectures at community events/conferences directed to patients and families, consumers, support groups, etc. Website, online, other media **Publications** (hard copy required, abstract accepted if text more than 25 pages) **Marketing materials**, brochures, flyers showing applicant's contribution are acceptable **Summary letters, handouts,** Slide handouts; course/conference evaluation comments and ratings are valuable Other, documentation prepared by applicant Research Funded or Unfunded Publications Awards and/or Honors Special recognitions	Evidence of patient/family and/or client teaching required for credential award; Evidence of education of consumers and other community groups valuable; Evidence of education of other professionals valuable Summaries of proposals and reports, abstracts Certificates, letters (copies accepted); hard copy of publications (summaries if text over 25 pages)	

Curriculum Vitae: Required Components

All components listed below must be present in the Curriculum Vitae (CV).
The applicant is urged to arrange the components of the CV in the order listed.

1. Full Legal Name
2. Last four digits of Social Security Number
3. Date of Birth
4. Place of Birth
5. Home Address, Telephone, Fax, and Email (if applicable)
6. Title (Professional Role)
7. Organization
8. Work Address, Telephone, Fax, and Email
9. Education (Dates of attendance, degrees or certificates, fields of study, organizations, locations)
10. Certifications (Dates, Certificate Name in full, Organizations, Locations)
11. Professional Positions (Dates of employment, titles, organizations, locations; summary of responsibilities). **NOTE:** ALL POSITIONS MUST BE DESCRIBED (BRIEFLY) WITH PERCENT OF TIME DEVOTED TO CLINICAL CARE, EDUCATION/TEACHING, ADMINISTRATION, RESEARCH, AND/OR OTHER ACTIVITIES.
12. Academic Appointments (Dates of appointments to academic educational position, titles, organizations, locations; summary of responsibilities)
13. Professional Organization Memberships and Activities
14. Special Projects (if applicable)
15. Honors, Awards, Special Recognitions (if applicable)
16. Research Activities (please use full citations, Manual of the American Psychological Association [APA] style suggested)
17. Publications (please use full citations, APA style suggested)
18. Presentations (please use full citations, APA style suggested)
19. Community Memberships and Activities (Organization name in full, location)
20. Other (if applicable)

Statement of career goals and reason(s) for applying for APNG (maximum length ½ page)

CURRICULUM VITAE

MARY SMITH, MSN, RN

Nurse Specialist in Prenatal Genetics

Place of Birth:	Chicago, IL
Date of Birth:	1 January
Home Address:	
	1234 Town Avenue
	Smithville, VA 56789
	USA
Telephone:	987.654.3210

Title (Professional Role): Nurse Specialist in Prenatal Genetics

Organization:	ABC HEALTH SCIENCES CENTER
	Department of Obstetrics and Gynecology
	1 ABC HEALTH SCIENCES CENTER AVENUE
	FAIRFAX, VA 98765

Telephone:	1.234.567.8901
Fax:	1.234.345.6789
Email:	marysmith@abc.edorg

Education:

1993	BS in Nursing, University of America, Fairfax, VA
1998	MS in Nursing, University of America, Fairfax, VA

Certificates: Certified Breast Feeding Consultant, 1995

Professional Experience:

1993-98	Staff Nurse and Unit Supervisor, Obstetrics ABC HEALTH SCIENCES CENTER, Fairfax, VA 98765 100% Clinical Nursing
1998 – present	Prenatal Genetics Nurse Specialist, ABC HEALTH SCIENCES CENTER 80% Clinical Nursing in Prenatal Genetics (Client and family assessment, counseling, case coordination); 10% Professional and community education outreach (supervise BSN students, provide in-service and professional lectures and consumer education programs to lay and community groups in the Fairfax, VA area); 10% Clinical Research (J. Doe, PhD, RN, Principal Investigator)

Academic Appointments
1998 – present   Clinical Preceptor, School of Nursing
                   (supervise senior BSN students in Community Health Nursing)
                   ABC HEALTH SCIENCES CENTER, Fairfax, VA 98765

Professional Organization
1994 – present   Member, Virginia Nurses Association, Ethics Committee
1998 – present   Member, International Society of Nursing in Genetics
                   Secretary, Professional Practice and Standards Committee

Special Recognitions
      2003   ABC Health Sciences Center Nurse of the Year

Research
2002 – 2004   Co-investigator, Attitudes toward prenatal testing therapy among
                   pregnant women with thalassemia (funded by ABC School of
                   Medicine intramural grant, $14,500)

Publications
Smith, M. (1998). Teaching breast feeding to adolescent mothers. Journal of
      Breastfeeding, 10, 240-243.

Presentations

Allan, A., & Smith, M. (October, 1995). Basics of breastfeeding. Virginia Nurses
      Association Conference on Women's Health. Fairfax, VA.

Smith, M. (April, 1996). Breastfeeding and premature infants . Virginia Nurses
      Association Annual Convention and Educational Program. Fairfax, VA.

Smith, M. & George, P. (June, 1997). Prenatal care for women with thalassemia.
      Virginia League of Nursing Conference. Richmond, VA.

Smith, M. (June, 2001). Prenatal diagnosis for women with hemoglobinopthies. Virginia
      League of Nursing Conference. Richmond, VA.

Smith, M. (October, 2003). Basics of prenatal therapies. Virginia Nurses Association
      Conference on Women's Health. Virginia Beach, VA.

Gollins, J., Doe J., &, Smith, M. (October, 1998). Basics of prenatal genetic diagnosis.
      Virginia Nurses Association Annual Convention and Educational Program. Virginia
      Beach, VA.

Gollins, J., & Doe, M. (May, 1999). Preimplantation technologies and infertile women.
      Association of Women's Health, Obstetrical, and Neonatal Nursing Educational
      Program. Richmond, VA.

Millioning, M., & Doe, M. (October, 2002). Basics of gene-based therapies. Virginia
      Nurses Association Annual Convention and Educational Program. Virginia Beach, VA.

<u>Statement of Career Goals and Reason(s) for Applying for APNG</u>

One of my goals in my nursing career is to become certified in nursing in the area of my chosen specialty, clinical genetics, especially in the field of prenatal and perinatal nursing. I have been a nurse for over 10 years, and nearly all of my experience has been in obstetrical nursing working with new mothers, infants, and their families and working with pregnant women and their families. I personally have seen the heartbreak of women coping with infertility and families who have had a child with a birth defect or a genetic diagnosis.

I feel that my Masters in Nursing has prepared me to become an expert nurse and a compassionate clinical professional. I have learned most of my knowledge about genetics after graduating from my Masters Program and practicing in Prenatal Genetics. I feel that I have had very valuable experiences working with my colleagues at the ABC Health Sciences Center and have had many opportunities to attend continuing education programs in the field of prenatal genetics. Also, I have had three online courses in genetics (from the March of Dimes, from the University of Iowa, and from the National Coalition for Health Professional Education in Genetics) totaling over 100 hours of my personal time over the past three years.

I feel that I am ready to qualify for the APNG because of my experience and my educational background. I know that this credential will signify to my patients and families and to my professional colleagues that I am dedicated to being the best nurse in my chosen field as possible. I hope that my portfolio will show that I deserve the APNG.

Verification Statement from Employer/Supervisor/Professional Colleague
Validating the Log and Case Studies Submitted by the Applicant for
the Advanced Practice Nurse in Genetics Credential *

Date:

To: Genetic Nursing Credentialing Commission

From:

To the best of my knowledge, I verify that the case log and case studies submitted by
_____ (Applicant's Name) reflect this individual's genetic nursing
practice and that he/she has provided health care to the clients listed and described in the
attached Portfolio of evidence for the Advanced Practice Nurse in Genetics credential.

Signed _____

Title:

Organization:

Location:

Tel:
Fax:
Email

* This statement must be on organization or agency letterhead, sealed in envelope with signature on flap. It is
subject to verification by the Genetic Nursing Credentialing Commission Score Team

ABC HEALTH SCIENCES CENTER
Department of Obstetrics and Gynecology
1 ABC HEALTH SCIENCES CENTER AVENUE
FAIRFAX, VA 98765

Date: 1 January 2004

To: Genetic Nursing Credentialing Commission

From: Gerold G. Geneticist, MD, PhD, FACOG, FACMG

To the best of my knowledge, I verify that the case log and case studies submitted by
_____Mary Smith, MSN, RN_____ (Applicant's Name) reflect this individual's genetic
nursing practice and that he/she has provided health care to the clients listed and
described in the attached Portfolio of evidence for the Advanced Practice Nurse in
Genetics credential.

Signed _____

Title: Medical Director, Obstetrics and Gynecology

Organization: ABC HEALTH SCIENCES CENTER
                Department of Obstetrics and Gynecology
                1 ABC HEALTH SCIENCES CENTER AVENUE
                FAIRFAX, VA 98765

Tel: 123.456.7890
Fax: 987.654.3210
Email: ggg@abc.edorg

INTERNATIONAL SOCIETY OF NURSES IN GENETICS CREDENTIALING PROGRAM
PROFESSIONAL PERFORMANCE VERIFICATION & EVALUATION FORM FOR THE APNG
PEER REVIEW—Three separate ratings required; sealed in envelopes w/signatures on flaps

---

1. Participates in practice improvement activities such as: participating actively in performance self appraisal process and obtaining feedback from patients.
   __Always__   Consistently   Sometimes   Rarely   Never

2. Seeks consultation and feedback from peers regarding clinical practice and role performance.
   __Always__   Consistently   Sometimes   Rarely   Never

3. Attends conferences, and other educational activities relevant to practice to acquire and maintain knowledge
   Always   ***Consistently***   Sometimes   Rarely   Never

4. Provides academic lectures and in-service presentations to peers and colleagues
   Always   ***Consistently***   Sometimes   Rarely   Never

5. Provides care and services in an objective non-judgmental and non-discriminatory manner.
   __Always__   Consistently   Sometimes   Rarely   Never

6. Professional decision-making and interactions with patients and colleagues reflect an ethical framework.
   __Always__   Consistently   Sometimes   Rarely   Never

7. Collaborates with patient / patient's family and other care providers in delivery of health care & services.
   __Always__   Consistently   Sometimes   Rarely   Never

8. Assists patient and family in identifying and obtaining available and appropriate services
   __Always__   Consistently   Sometimes   Rarely   Never

9. Develops, conducts and /or critiques clinical research
   Always   ***Consistently***   Sometimes   Rarely   Never

I verify, to the best of my knowledge that Ms. Mary Smith, MSN, RN *(applicant's name)* has performed according to the above ratings and has provided care to the clients and families documented in the accompanying case studies and case log.

Name John Doe, PhD, RN, APNG Signature: _____
Title Clinical Director of Genetic Services
Organization ABC Health Sciences Center   Date 01.25.2004
Contact information (in the event of validation by the Genetic Nursing Credentialing Commission):
Tel: 1.234.567.8901 Fax: 211.345.6789 Email: johndoe@abc.edorg
Length of time you have interacted professionally: six years
Relationship/capacity of professional interaction: team leader and colleague
Your additional comments are welcome:
Ms. Smith is a very competent and dedicated nursing professional. She is consistently accurate and caring with patients and families in our clinic. She receives high ratings on her performance evaluations every year, and has demonstrated an outstanding record of service to her professional organization and to her community.

1. Participates in practice improvement activities such as: participating actively in performance self appraisal process and obtaining feedback from patients.

   Always   Consistently   Sometimes   Rarely   Never

2. Seeks consultation and feedback from peers regarding clinical practice and role performance.

   Always   Consistently   Sometimes   Rarely   Never

3. Attends conferences, grand rounds and other educational activities relevant to practice to acquire and maintain knowledge

   Always   Consistently   Sometimes   Rarely   Never

4. Provides academic lectures and in-service presentations to peers and colleagues

   Always   Consistently   Sometimes   Rarely   Never

5. Provides care and services in an objective non-judgmental and non-discriminatory manner.

   Always   Consistently   Sometimes   Rarely   Never

6. Professional decision-making and interactions with patients and colleagues reflect an ethical framework.

   Always   Consistently   Sometimes   Rarely   Never

7. Collaborates with patient / patient's family and other care providers in delivery of health care & services.

   Always   Consistently   Sometimes   Rarely   Never

8. Assists patient and family in identifying and obtaining available and appropriate services

   Always   Consistently   Sometimes   Rarely   Never

9. Develops, conducts and /or critiques clinical research

   Always   Consistently   Sometimes   Rarely   Never

I verify, to the best of my knowledge that _____ *(applicant's name)* has performed according to the above ratings and has provided care to the clients and families documented in the accompanying case studies and case log.

Name_____ Signature: _____
Title_____
Organization_____ Date_____
Contact information (in the event of validation by the Genetic Nursing Credentialing Commission):
Tel: _____ Fax: _____ Email:
Length of time you have interacted professionally:
Relationship/capacity of professional interaction:
Your additional comments are welcome:

Appendix C
Selected Components of the GNCC Portfolio Evaluation and Scoring Training Manual

As discussed in detail in Chapter 6, the training of the GNCC Score Teams rests upon explicit guidelines for the evaluation of portfolios, examples of which are included in this appendix. (Included also are sample pages from a fictitious GNCC portfolio.) Such evaluation entails on-site retreats as well as individual study and commitment by Score Team members to fairly appraise the applicant's submissions for the APNG and GCN credentials. Score Teams include clinicians, educators, and nurses in related roles with a breath of experience in genetics health care as well as nursing education.

The portfolio scoring system covers several areas or categories of content, all of which are based upon *Statement on the Scope and Standards of Genetics Clinical Nursing Practice* (ANA and ISONG, 1998).

The complete *Portfolio Evaluation and Scoring Training Manual* contains the following information:

- Timeline from training to the final retreat and credential recommendation
- Guidelines and ethical standards
- How to grade the portfolio
- Neural net portfolio statistical analysis information
- Glossary
- Sample neural net software web site scoring pages
- Genetic Nursing Credentialing Commission (GNCC) By-Laws
- Members of the GNCC Committee and the GNCC Score Team
- Portfolio application guidelines packet
- Samples of selected pages from previously submitted portfolios with reviewing scorers commentary

Chapters 4 and 6 contain more details about both the application packet and this training manual.

GNCC
GENETIC NURSING
CREDENTIALING COMMISSION

GENETIC NURSING
CREDENTIALING COMMISSION

PORTFOLIO
EVALUATION
AND SCORING
TRAINING
MANUAL

2004–5 Edition

GNCC logo by Jason Greco (DNA picture courtesy of DOE Human Genome Program http://www.ornl.gov/hgmis)

GUIDELINES AND ETHICAL STANDARDS FOR SCORE TEAMS

The portfolio process is the method used by the Genetic Nursing Credentialing Commission (GNCC) to determine the qualifications of nurse applicants for the Advanced Practice Nurse in Genetics credential (APNG) and the Genetics Clinical Nurse credential (GCN).

This training manual will serve to provide guidelines and reference points to the APNG and the GCN Score Teams. The manual, although written for the purposes of preparing the Score Teams, is a "work-in-progress" that must be responsive to the growing genetic concerns of patients, families, and communities; the evolving nature of nursing and health care; and the development of education and expertise in nurse clinicians in a wide variety of settings.

The GNCC has established the policies and procedures for portfolio evaluation and scoring in this training manual. It is primarily directed to the members of the Score Teams, but may serve as a resource for other individuals or groups interested in the portfolio evaluation process. In addition, this manual is expected to serve as an adjunct to the processes for future development of certification for nurses not only in genetic health care settings, but also in settings in which genetic concerns arise as nurses care for the entire spectrum of consumers of health care.

The integrity of the portfolio evaluation and scoring process and the necessary protection and respect due to individual credential applicants depends upon the following principles:

1. All transactions and discussions of individual portfolio evaluation and scoring are confidential.
2. No Score Team member or leader may divulge any part of individual portfolio contents to anyone other than other team members, leaders, or GNCC officers. Individual nurse applicants may have access to the written records associated only with their own portfolio contents via written permission of the President of the GNCC or his/her designee.
3. The individual applicant has the right to due process in the event of failure to achieve a passing score on the portfolio, disputes or questions regarding the portfolio final score, or related questions associated with the evaluation and scoring procedures.

Due process will consist of a) written request for review and reason(s) for review directed to the officers of the GNCC; b) review of the portfolio contents, the evaluation and scoring records, and other pertinent materials by an impartial panel assembled from within the GNCC (i.e., an alternate Score Team trained in evaluation and scoring procedures); and c) written response to the request from the officers of the GNCC. Legal consultation will be used if/when resolution of review cannot be achieved by either the GNCC or the individual applicant.

ALL SCORE TEAM MEMBERS WILL MAINTAIN A LOG OF THEIR WORK TO ENSURE AUDITABILITY AND ACCURACY OF FINDINGS. Score Team member logs will be used in the event of questions, computer file problems, data analysis checks, and related concerns.

PORTFOLIO SCORING PROCESS

Timeline

September 1	Call for Portfolios
March 1	Deadline for submission of Portfolios

Receive and review portfolios for completeness by President of the GNCC or his or her designee.

Incomplete portfolios are returned to applicant with explanation of missing items and instructions for resubmission.

Once Portfolio is determined to be complete and ready for scoring, ports will be mailed to Score Team. Expect to begin receiving portfolios during mid-May to early June

June - July	Score Team Review, Score & submit scores to CSL website
July - August	Score team reviews Scoring Report and decides who passes / fails. Original portfolios are returned for archival storage with the GNCC, copies of portfolios are destroyed by the President of the GNCC or his or her designee
September – November	Successful candidates receive credential; unsuccessful candidates receive notification that they have not passed and can resubmit, if eligible

General Suggestions & Guidelines

1. Read and score the portfolios as they come in; do not wait to read them all at once.
2. We recommend that you score no more than one portfolio at one sitting.
3. It is estimated that each portfolio will take between 2 and 3 hours to score.
4. In the event your score is challenged or you need to refer to your analysis of an individual portfolio, we suggest you make short notes or comments as you go along indicating your thoughts.
5. Before you start scoring a portfolio, we recommend you have the following items nearby (see following pages in this guideline packet):
   ISONG and ANA Standards Genetics Clinical Nursing Practice & Performance Indicators; a copy of the GNCC Application Guidelines Packet
   Component requirements
   Two versions of Portfolio Scoring Guides "Cheat Sheet"
   Continuing education contact hourse equivalency table
6. Use whatever method you feel is most comfortable for you, i.e. use ISONG standards, Performance indicators, Scoring Guide, etc.
7. You may wish to refer to the Application Guidelines Packet as you are reviewing a portfolio to compare the contents to the directions given to the applicant.

Where do I begin and how do I score a portfolio?

- Open portfolio packet and separate into component parts
  - CV
  - Peer & Professional Performance
  - Case Studies
  - Case Log
  - Formal / Informal Education supporting documents
  - Evidence of research
  - Evidence of patient. Professional or Community education
  - Special recognition
  - Publications

Be sure that the applicant for the APNG has a Bachelor's degree in nursing and Master's degree in nursing or equivalent (Masters in a related field accepted till 2005) or that the applicant for the GCN has a Bachelor's degree in nursing or equivalent (Bachelor's in a related field accepted till 2006).

- **Enter applicant name and special identification # on Portfolio Scoring Guide** (see next pages, be sure to use correct page for applicant, i.e., APNG or GCN form)

- **CV**   Among other observations,
  - Does the applicant list major responsibilities with each position?
  - Are you able to determine that applicant has 3 years experience as a genetic nurse in which greater than 50% of the job responsibilities require applied use of genetic knowledge.
  - Does applicant have certification in other areas of expertise?
  - Has applicant been active in a related professional association? This can generally be ascertained by committee / organization responsibilities / leadership.

- **Formal education transcripts**
  - Are the transcripts original? (There will be a notation on your copy of the transcript authenticating its coming in a sealed envelope w/Registrar's mark on the flap)
  - Undergraduate program: range of courses? Grades?
  - Master's program: relevant to their field of practice? Genetic content (SEE BOX ON THE NEXT PAGE)

- **Informal Education:**
  - Are continuing education contact hours within 5 years of application?
  - Relate to human genetics?
  - Quality of Education: i.e. are they all derived from individual computer based training modules or are they short courses offered by a reputable academic institution? Level I, Level II or Level III?
  - Does applicant demonstrate a commitment to improving his/her genetic knowledge base?
  - Is there evidence of 50 contact hours of genetic based continuing education?

CEU Equivalency Table (from ANCC *Certification Guide*)

Unit of Education	IS EQUAL TO
1 CEU	10 Contact Hours
1 Contact hour	0.1 CEU or 50 clock minutes
1 Academic semester	15 Contact hours
1 Academic quarter	12.5 Contact hours
1 CME	1.2 Contact hours or 60 clock minutes

REQUIRED COURSE CONTENT
Human Genetics
Molecular and Biochemical Genetics
Ethical, Legal, and Social Issues
Clinical Applications of Genetics including Genetic Counseling Genetic Variations in Populations

- **Case Logs**
  - Are 50 cases included? Do cases represent a single diagnosis or are diverse cases represented within the specialty?
  - Does Case Log demonstrate the delivery of individualized genetic health care to patients? It is not realistic that all patients need a homogeneous approach in the delivery of genetic health care.
  - Are the case logs validated by a supervisor?
  - What is the role of the supervisor? Is this person a genetic professional or a professional capable of judging the care delivered by the applicant? Is the signatory a business manager or administrative assistant?
- **Performance appraisal / Peer evaluations**
  (judging ISONG Professional Standards)
  - Is the applicant rated consistently high with no variance?
  - Is the appraiser in a position to professionally assess the applicant?
  - Are any weaknesses evident? Are these weaknesses of significance?
  - Has the appraiser made any comments or remarks that influence your judgement?
- **Case Studies**
  - Did the applicant submit 4 case studies?
  - Are the case studies identifiable as coming from the Case Log?
  - Do the case studies reflect ethical conduct by the applicant?
  - Are identifiers present?   Were patients identified by name?
  - Does a minimum 3-generation pedigree accompany each case study?
  - Is the pedigree consistent with history provided?
  - Is the pedigree consistent with standard practice in clinical genetic services?
  - Are the personal and family histories comprehensive and understandable?
  - Are the Case Studies in Modified SOAPIER format?
  - Are the diagnoses offered medical or nursing diagnoses?
  - Are the nursing diagnoses consistent with information provided?
  - Are the nursing interventions appropriate based on the information provided?
  - Are you able to determine the applicants' communication or writing abilities?
  - Can you determine if the applicant respected and supported the client's decisions?
  - Are patient teaching materials included? Are they appropriate and understandable?
  - Is there documentation of genetic risk (APNG) or need for referral to genetic services (GCN)?
  - Are you able to determine that psychosocial issues were explored and addressed?

After a thorough review of each section, you are to decide the level of competency you think the applicant demonstrates in that particular area.

The applicant's practice according to the documentation provided:
- exceeds the ISONG Standards of Practice,
- meets the ISONG standard of practices,
- falls below the ISONG Standards of Practice, or
- falls well below the ISONG Standards of Practice.

The CSL program accepts a score between 4 and 10. The table below provides a guideline for you as you assign a number score for the section you reviewed. Using the table above as a guide, you **must** enter one of the following numbers that you believe reflects the level of competence the applicant demonstrates for that particular category.

SCORE	ASSESSMENT
9-10	Exceeds standards
7-8	Meets standards of Practice
5-6	Below standard
4	Well below standard

ALTHOUGH NOT INCLUDED IN THIS TEXT, THE MANUAL INCLUDES SEVERAL EXAMPLES OF PREVIOUSLY SUBMITTED PORTFOLIO CONTENTS THAT HAVE BEEN MASKED TO PROTECT THE IDENTITIES OF THE APPLICANTS AS WELL AS PATIENTS AND FAMILIES IN THE SECTIONS PERTAINING TO CLINICAL NURSING PRACTICE. THESE EXAMPLES HAVE BEEN RATED AND ARE USED IN THE TRAINING OF SCORE TEAMS

Index

National Association of Clinical Nurse Specialists (NACNS), 29
National Board for Professional Teaching Standards (NBPTS), 36
National Council of State Boards of Nursing (NCSBN), 25, 57
National Institutes of Health, Office of Biotechnology Activities, 115
National Society of Genetic Counselors, 57
Neural net scoring program, 29, 49, 58, 74, 86–89
Novice-to-expert nursing model, viii, 18
Nursing: portfolios in, 17–18, 27–34, 41; Web site resources for portfolios in, 51
Nursing and Midwifery Council (NMC), 30–31
Nursing education: in genetics, 55–56; portfolios in, 16–17

O

Occupational therapy, portfolios in, 35
Oermann, M., 26
Oklahoma Board of Nursing, 27–28
Organization of portfolios, 12, 44

P

Pattern recognition program. *See* Neural net scoring program
Pedigree symbols, 92
Performance-based evaluations, 3–4, 8
Performance indicators, 59–63, 82–84, 113–15
Personal development plan, 30
Personal Professional Profile, 30–31
Pew Health Professions Commission, 46
Portfolio Evaluation and Scoring Training Manual, 70, 72, 74; selected components of, 133–38
Portfolio evaluation process: components of standards for, 81; development of, 80–81; indicators of satisfactory accomplishment for, 82–84; neural net scoring program for, 86–89; reviewers in, 85–86; scoring in, 84; standards for, 80–81; teamwork for, 79–80
Portfolios: characteristics of, 12–14; components of, 41, 42; definition of, 11; as evaluation method, 5, 8–9, 18; growth versus best-work, 9, 26; overview of, xiii–xiv; profiles versus, 26; uses of, 25–36. *See also* Portfolio evaluation process
Postregistration education and practice (PREP) standards, 30

Practical knowledge: evaluation of, vii–viii; importance of, viii–ix; transmission of, viii
Practice settings, key attributes of, 34
Preparation of portfolio, value of, 27
Presentations, documenting, 42
Prior learning credit, 17
Privacy Rules of the Health Insurance Portability and Accountability Act (HIPPA), 46
Professional development, through portfolio preparation, 27
Professional Development Portfolio (PDP), 34–35
Professional Development Tool (PDT), 35
Profiles, 26, 30–31
Publications, documenting, 42
Purpose of portfolio, 43

Q

Qualitative methods, 7

R

Reflection: journals for, 14; reflection-in-action, 17; reflection-on-action, 17; role in portfolios of, 13–14; self-reflection, 17; types of, 33
Reliability of evaluation methods, 6–7; portfolios, 18, 58
Retreats, Score Team, 73–75
Role performance, documenting, 64
Royal College of Nursing (RCN), United Kingdom, 32

S

Scope and Standards of Genetics Clinical Nursing Practice, xiv, 56
Scope and Standards of Nursing Practice, 56, 59
Score Teams, 69–78, 85–86; debriefing, 75–76; guidelines and ethics for, 76–78; qualifications of, 69–70; retreats for, 73–75; scoring processes of, 71–75; training of, 70–76
Scoring, 71–75, 84. *See also* Neural net scoring program
Screening standards, 81–82
Selectivity of portfolios, 13
Self-evaluations, 3–4
Self-reflection, 17
Standards for credentials, 81–82; components of, 82; evaluative, 81–82; screening, 81–82